MW00342607

Church of the Holy House at Loretto
where Crashaw lies buried.

Church of the Holy House at Loretto
where Crashaw lies buried.

E. H. Palmer
11 Quing oth.
1902

THE
ENGLISH POEMS
of
RICHARD
CRASHAW

EDITED, *WITH AN INTRODUCTION & NOTES*

By EDWARD HUTTON

WITH A FRONTISPIECE

LONDON
METHUEN & CO.
36 ESSEX STREET W.C.
MDCCCCI

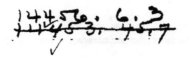

TO THE

DEAR and SWEET MEMORY

OF

NICHOLAS FERRAR

Who died at Little Gidding
Dec. 4, 1637

Being ADVENT SUNDAY

This Edition of the POEMS of his Friend

RICHARD CRASHAW

is dedicated

Requiem aeternam dona eis, Domine
et lux perpetua luceat eis

CONTENTS

	Page
Introduction	xi

STEPS TO THE TEMPLE

The Weeper	3
Sancta Maria Dolorum	12
The Tear	16
The Office of Holy Cross	19
Vexilla Regis	32
Neither durst any man ask Him any more questions	34
On the Wounds of our Crucified Lord	35
Upon the Bleeding Crucifix	36
To the Name above every Name	38
Psalm XXIII	46
Psalm CXXXVII	48
In the Holy Nativity of our Blessed Lord	50
A Hymn for the Circumcision of our Blessed Lord	55
Our Blessed Lord in His Circumcision to His Father	56
To the Queen's Majesty—a Dedication	58
In the Glorious Epiphany of our Blessed Lord	59
Upon Easter Day	70
Sospetto d'Herode	71
Hymn of St. Thomas	97
Lauda Sion Salvatorem	99
Prayer : an Ode prefixed to a little Prayer-Book	103
To the Same	107
A Description of a Religious House	109
On Mr. George Herbert's Book	110
A Hymn to St. Teresa	111
An Apology for the Foregoing	117
The Flaming Heart	119
A Song of Divine Love	123

E, H, Salmon
11 Leamington.
1902

CONTENTS

	Page
An Epitaph on a Young Married Couple . .	179
Death's Lecture and the Funeral of a Young Gentleman	179
An Epitaph on Dr. Brook	181
On a Foul Morning	181
To the Morning	182
Love's Horoscope	184
Upon the Frontispiece of Mr. Isaacson's Chronology	186
To the Queen	187
To the Queen, on her numerous progeny . .	188
Upon two green apricots sent to Mr. Cowley .	194
Alexias	195

TRANSLATIONS

In praise of spring (Virgil)	200
The beginning of Heliodorus . . .	201
Cupid's Crier (Greek)	202
To thy lover, A Song (Italian) . . .	205
Love now no fire (Italian)	207
Would any one (Italian)	207
Come let us live (Catullus)	208

EPIGRAMS

Upon Ford's two tragedies	208
On Marriage	209
On the Fair Ethiopian	209
To Delia, out of Martial	209
Upon Venus putting on Mars' arms . .	209
Upon the same	210
On Nanus mounted upon an ant . . .	210
Temperance	210
Crashaw's answer to Cowley, on Hope . .	212
Crashaw's Motto	214

E. H. Palmer
11 Quincy St.
1902

He who had known Nicholas Ferrar at Little Gidding, and lived in that quiet and monastic household, could never quite have reconciled himself to disputes or arguings, or to the practical makeshifts of the less severe and perfect society of the world.   Already he is friends with Thomas Shelford, a Peterhouse man, and parson of Kingsfield in Suffolk, who has gone so far (a far way indeed in those days) as to protest against the identification of the Pope with the antichrist.

. And here it may be well to suggest that Crashaw's religion does not seem to have been so much a matter about which it was possible to argue, not so much a matter of difference in belief or creed between the opinions he held when "he was among the Protestants" and after he became a Roman Catholic ; it does not seem to have been an act of faith, or credulity, so much as an attitude of mind, a colouring of his spirit that he was probably born with, and that no amount of fortune, good or bad, no influence exercised by his father over him could ever have changed.   He was born to appreciate and care strongly for those things which the Romanists, as distinct from any other body of Christians, express most perfectly.   And so when, on 21st December 1642, the Chapel of Peterhouse was sacked by the Rebels, and the Parliament Commissioners insisted on all the Fellows taking the oath to the League and Covenant, Crashaw, with five others, declined and with them was expelled. The inevitable had happened, and he was free for a few months before he was to submit himself to the Roman Church.

He went to Paris. Perhaps because Cowley was there, perhaps because Queen Henrietta Maria, the beautiful wife of Charles I., was there too in exile. Indeed Crashaw seems always to have entertained a romantic affection for this unhappy lady, so that he wrote her many poems, and counts her children as though they were precious to him for her sake. Cowley, a friend whom he had known for ten years, seems to have found him in Paris in great distress, but a Roman Catholic at last, writing letters in verse to his patron, Susan Fielding, Countess of Denbigh, sister of the great Duke of Buckingham, urging her to follow him into the Roman Church.

And at last, mainly owing to Cowley's efforts, he was brought to the Queen, who sent him to the Cardinal Palotta in Rome, and being a Queen, with a purse of gold, the gift of Her Majesty.

It was probably in 1648 that he set out for Italy, going by sea, one may suppose, from Marseilles to Genoa or Civita Vecchia, as Evelyn had already done. The Cardinal, who appears to have somewhat patronised him, and yet not unkindly, gave him no better office than that of attendant or secretary. But the Italians seem to have been in his

eyes as great enemies to the spiritual life as the
Puritans, though probably in a different way; and so
we find Crashaw complaining of the acts of his
fellow-servants to the Cardinal, whose ear he is
supposed to have had.   For his own safety after
that, the Cardinal sent him to Loretto as a Canon
of the Chapel of Our Lady there.   Starting from
Rome as a pilgrim in summer time, he caught fever
by the way and died four weeks after coming to
Loretto, where he lies buried.

It would be unwise within the limits of a short
introduction to try in any way to sum up Crashaw's
work, and "place" him in the national collection
of poets.   It will be sufficient to notice a few of
the characteristics of his verse.   It is, then, let me
say at the very outset, beyond the religious poetry
of any of his contemporaries.   He has passion and a
great gift of sincerity.   By that it is not meant that
he merely means what he says, but that he is artist
enough to be able to be sincere in reality and to ap-
pear sincere.   The loveliness of his imagination is
often too luxuriant, but often so delicate and simple
as to remind one of the best work of the lyric poets
of the preceding age.   These verses from "In the
Holy Nativity," for instance, have the touch of the
falling snow itself, so delicate are they:

> "I saw the curled drops, soft and slow,
> Come hovering o'er the place's head;
> Offering their whitest sheets of snow
> To furnish the fair Infant's bed:

Forbear, said I; be not too bold,
Your fleece is white, but 'tis too cold.

I saw the obsequious Seraphim
Their rosy fleece of fire bestow,
  For well they now can spare their wing,
Since Heaven itself lies here below.
  Well done, said I, but are you sure
Your down so warm, will pass for pure?

No, no, your King's not yet to seek
Where to repose His royal head;
  See, see, how soon His new-bloom'd cheek
'Twixt's Mother's breasts is gone to bed.
  Sweet choice, said we, no way but so
Not to lie cold, yet sleep in snow."

Another example of his perfection of phrase may
be given, to compare with which I can find nothing
in Herbert or Vaughan:

"The dew no more will sleep
  Nuzzled in the lilies' neck."

But it is never or seldom he is at his best all
through a long poem. In "The Flaming Heart,"
for instance, he is involved, difficult, full of conceits
for two-thirds of the poem, breaking out at last,
however, into one of the most glorious lyrical
passages in the language. This ending is indeed a
very litany, an invocation so swift, so impassioned,

b

as to carry one away and make one forget that the
greater part of the poem was mere verse :

"O thou undaunted daughter of desires!
  By all thy dower of lights and fires;
  By all the eagle in thee, all the dove;
  By all thy lives and deaths of love;
  By thy large draughts of intellectual day,
  And by thy thirsts of love more large than they;
  By all thy brim-fill'd bowls of fierce desire,
  By thy last morning's draught of liquid fire;
  By the full kingdom of that final kiss
  That seized thy parting soul, and seal'd thee His;
  By all the Heaven thou hast in Him
  (Sweet sister of the Seraphim!)
  By all of Him we have in thee;
  Leave nothing of myself in me.
  Let me so read thy life, that I
  Unto all life of mine may die."

Perhaps, however, the finest of his poems as a
whole is the "Hymn to the Name and Honour of
St. Teresa," to which "The Flaming Heart" is
a kind of postscript. It never sinks below the
level of poetry; it is often poetry of a high order,
and the intolerable conceits of some of his pieces
are altogether absent. This piece was written
"when he was yet among the Protestants," as
he explains in a very charming apology to St.
Teresa for having invoked her name while still
a "heretic."

   "The Weeper," a poem on St. Mary Magdalene,

is the most fantastic of his poems; it is full of the most intolerable conceits and petty sillinesses, and yet at times is so marvellously delicate that, as Mr. Saintsbury has somewhere well said, "only Blake in a few snatches has ever equalled" these verses.

It will be seen, then, that Crashaw is occasionally, and not so rarely after all, beyond any religious poet in the English language, and on the other hand occasionally below even some of the more tiresome gush of Herbert. He is never dull, and even at his worst one may be sure of a delightful surprise in a few lines if one will only have the patience to read on. And withal, there are few men in all literature more lovable. It is the effect, I think, of his sincerity. To him the Virgin is a lady of some great romance, a Princess whom he worships afar off. In Saint Teresa he has a more terrible joy; she appears to him as a great warrior Saint, an "undaunted daughter," and the influence of her books is, I venture to think, clearly visible in Crashaw's work.

The intellectual imagination was the chief characteristic of Richard Crashaw, and it is with a perfect confidence of his immortality in literature we may say:

"If you think
'Tis but a dead face Art doth here bequeath,
Look on the following leaves, and see him breathe."

The text of this edition of Crashaw's poems is chiefly that of 1648, in which year *Steps to the Temple* was issued in a second edition with pieces not before printed.

I have to acknowledge, like every other student of seventeenth-century poetry, my indebtedness to the Rev. A. B. Grosart for his edition, privately printed in 1873, of *The Complete Works of Crashaw*. That is nearly thirty years ago now. Since then Mr. J. R. Tutin has done good service in printing *The English Poems of Richard Crashaw*. His is, I think, the only edition even professing to be complete, that has been issued since 1873.

To Dr. Garnett, C.B., I am indebted for notes 2, 3, 5, 9 on page 89, and for note 3, page 90, also for great kindness and courtesy on many occasions. Below is given a list of the English poems not included in this volume. They may be found in Rev. A. B. Grosart's edition in the British Museum, and in the Tanner MSS. in the Bodleian Library.

Pieces not included from the Tanner MSS.

Sacred Poems—

(1) Mary seeking Jesus when lost.
(2) The wounds of our Lord Jesus.
(3) On the Gunpowder Plot (three pieces).
(4) Out of Grotius' Tragedy of Christ's sufferings.

Secular Poems—

(1) Upon the King's (Charles I.) coronation.
(2)   ,,   ,,   ,,   ,,   ,,
(3) Upon the birth of the Princess Elizabeth.
(4) Upon a gnat burnt in a candle.
(5) From Petronius.
(6) From Horace (Ille et ne fasto te posuit die).
(7) Ex Euphormione.
(8) Elegy on the Death of Mr. Stanninow.
(9) Upon the Death of a friend.
(10) An Elegy on the Death of Dr. Porter.
(11) "At the ivory tribunal of your hand."
(12) "Though 'tis neither May nor June."

I

STEPS

TO THE

TEMPLE

Sacred Poems

With
The Delights of the Muses

By RICHARD CRASHAW, *some-
times of* Pembroke Hall *and
late fellow of* S. Peter's *Coll.*
in Cambridge

---

*The second Edition wherein are added divers
pieces not before extant*

LONDON
Printed for *Humphrey Moseley* and are to be
sold at his shop at the Princes Armes
in St. *Pauls* Church-yard
1648.

SAINT MARY MAGDALENE, OR, THE WEEPER

Lo! where a wounded heart with bleeding eyes conspire,
Is she a flaming fountain or a weeping fire?

THE WEEPER

I

Hail, sister springs!
　Parents of silver-footed rills!
Ever-bubbling things!
Thawing crystal! snowy hills
Still spending, never spent! I mean
Thy fair eyes, sweet Magdalene!

II

Heavens thy fair eyes be;
Heavens of ever-falling stars.
'Tis seed-time still with thee;
And stars thou sow'st, whose harvest dares
Promise the Earth to countershine
Whatever makes Heaven's forehead fine.

III

But we are deceivèd all :
Stars indeed they are too true :
For they but seem to fall,
As Heaven's other spangles do ;
It is not for our Earth and us,
To shine in things so precious.

IV

Upwards thou dost weep,
Heaven's bosom drinks the gentle stream.
Where th' milky rivers creep,
Thine floats above, and is the cream.
Waters above th' heavens, what they be
We are taught best by thy tears and thee.

V

Every morn from hence,
A brisk cherub something sips,
Whose sacred influence
Adds sweetness to his sweetest lips ;
Then to his music ; and his song
Tastes of this breakfast all day long.

VI

When some new bright guest
Takes up among the stars a room,
And Heaven will make a feast :
Angels with crystal phials [1] come
And draw from these full eyes of thine,
Their Master's water, their own wine.

[1] Original text, violls.

VII

The dew no more will weep
The primrose's pale cheek to deck :
The dew no more will sleep
Nuzzel'd [1] in the lily's neck ;
Much rather would it be thy tear,
And leave them both to tremble here.

VIII

Not the soft gold which
Steals from the amber-weeping tree,[2]
Makes Sorrow half so rich
As the drops distill'd from thee.
Sorrow's best jewels lie in these
Caskets, of which Heaven keeps the keys.

IX

When Sorrow would be seen
In her brightest majesty :
(For she is a Queen) :
Then is she dress'd by none but thee.
Then, and only then, she wears
Her proudest pearls : I mean, thy tears.

---

[1] Nestled.

[2] Obscure, possibly an evergreen shrub, a species of *Anthospermum*, whose leaves when bruised smell sweetly. But the tears of birds were said in old times to become amber. Cf. also *Othello*, v. 2—

> "Of one, whose subdued eyes . . .
> Drop tears as fast as the Arabian trees
> Their medicinal gum."

X

Not in the Evening's eyes,
When they red with weeping are
For the Sun that dies,
Sits Sorrow with a face so fair,
Nowhere but here did ever meet
Sweetness so sad, sadness so sweet.

XI

Sadness all the while
She sits in such a throne as this,
Can do nought but smile,
Nor believes she Sadness is :
Gladness itself would be more glad,
To be made so sweetly sad.

XII

There's no need at all,
That the balsam-sweating bough [1]
So coyly should let fall
His med'cinable tears ; for now
Nature has learnt to extract a dew
More sovereign and sweet, from you.

XIII

Yet let the poor drops weep,
(Weeping is the ease of Woe) :
Softly let them creep,
Sad that they are vanquish'd so.
They, though to others no relief,
Balsam may be for their own grief.

[1] A tree from which balsam is obtained, probably the *Abies balsamea.*

XIV

Golden though he be,
Golden Tagus murmurs through;
Were his way by thee,
Content and quiet he would go;
So much more rich would he esteem
'Thy silver, than his golden stream.

XV

Well does the May that lies
Smiling in thy cheeks, confess
The April in thine eyes;
Mutual sweetness they express.
No April e'er lent kinder showers,
Nor May returned more faithful flowers

XVI

O cheeks! Beds of chaste loves,
By your own showers seasonably dashed.
Eyes! Nests of milky doves,
In your own wells decently washed.
O wit of Love! that thus could place
Fountain and garden in one face.

XVII

O sweet contest of woes
With loves; of tears with smiles disputing!
O fair and friendly foes,
Each other kissing and confuting!
While rain and sunshine, cheeks and eyes,
Close in kind contrarieties.

XVIII

But can these fair floods be
Friends with the bosom-fires that fill thee?
Can so great flames agree
Eternal tears should thus distil thee?
O floods! O fires! O suns! O showers!
Mixed and made friends by Love's sweet powers.

XIX

'Twas His[1] well-pointed dart
That digged these wells, and dressed this wine;
And taught the wounded heart
The way into these weeping eyne.[2]
Vain loves avaunt![3] bold hands forbear!
The Lamb hath dipped His white foot here.

XX

And now where'er He stays,
Among the Galilean mountains,
Or more unwelcome ways;
He's followed by two faithful fountains;
Two walking baths, two weeping motions,
Portable, and compendious oceans.

XXI

O thou, thy Lord's fair store!
In thy so rich and rare expenses,
Even when He showed most poor
He might provoke the wealth of Princes.
What Prince's wanton'st pride e'er could
Wash with silver, wipe with gold?[4]

---

[1] Love's.   [2] Eyes.   [3] Away, begone.
[4] Gold, the Magdalene's hair.

XXII

Who is that King, but He
Who calls 't His crown, to be called thine,
That thus can boast to be
Waited on by a wandering mine,[1]
A voluntary mint, that strowes,
Warm silver showers where'er He goes?

XXIII

O precious prodigal!
Fair spendthrift of thyself! thy measure
(Merciless love!) is all.
Even to the last pearl in thy treasure:
All places, times, and objects be
Thy tears' sweet opportunity.

XXIV

Does the day-star rise?
Still thy tears do fall and fall.
Does Day close his eyes?
Still the fountain weeps for all.
Let Night or Day do what they will,
Thou hast thy task: thou weepest still.

XXV

Does thy song lull the air?
Thy falling tears keep faithful time.
Does thy sweet-breathed prayer
Up in clouds of incense climb?
Still at each sigh, that is each stop,
A bead, that is a tear, does drop.

[1] Mary's golden hair.

XXVI

At these thy weeping gates
(Watching their watery motion),
Each wingèd moment waits:
Takes his tear, and gets him gone.
By thine eyes' tinct [1] ennobled thus,
Time lays him up; he's precious.

XXVII

Time, as by thee He passes,
Makes thy ever-watery eyes
His hour-glasses.
By them His steps He rectifies.[2]
The sands He used no longer please,
For His own sands He'll use thy seas.

XXVIII

Not, "so long she livèd,"
Shall thy tomb report of thee;
But, "so long she grievèd":
Thus must we date thy memory.
Others by moments, months, and years
Measure their ages; thou, by tears.

XXIX

So do perfumes expire,
So sigh tormented sweets, opprest
With proud unpitying fire,
Such tears the suffering rose, that's vext
With ungentle flames, does shed,
Sweating in a too warm bed.

[1] Stain.   [2] He times his steps by her tears.

XXX

Say, ye bright brothers,
The fugitive sons of those fair eyes,
Your fruitful mothers,
What make you here? what hopes can 'tice [1]
You to be born? what cause can borrow
You from those nests of noble sorrow?

XXXI

Whither away so fast?
For sure the sluttish earth
Your sweetness cannot taste,
Nor does the dust deserve your birth.
Sweet, whither haste you then? O say
Why you trip so fast away?

XXXII

We go not to seek
The darlings of Aurora's bed,
The rose's modest cheek,
Nor the violet's humble head.
Though the field's eyes [2] too Weepers be,
Because they want such tears as we.

XXXIII

Much less mean we to trace
The fortune of inferior gems,
Preferr'd to some proud face,
Or perched upon fear'd diadems:
Crown'd heads are toys.   We go to meet
A worthy object, our Lord's feet.

[1] Entice.   [2] Flowers.

SANCTA MARIA DOLORUM, OR, THE MOTHER OF SORROWS

A PATHETICAL DESCANT UPON THE DEVOUT PLAIN-
SONG OF STABAT MATER DOLOROSA

I

IN shade of Death's sad tree [1]
    Stood doleful she.
Ah she, now by none other
Name to be known, alas, but Sorrow's Mother.
    Before her eyes
Hers and the whole World's Joy,
Hanging all torn, she sees ; and in His woes
And pains, her pangs and throes :
Each wound of His, from every part,
All more at home in her one heart.

II

What kind of marble then
    Is that cold man
    Who can look on and see,
Nor keep such noble sorrows company ?
    Sure even from you
    (My flints) [2] some drops are due,
To see so many unkind swords contest
    So fast for one soft breast :
While with a faithful, mutual flood,
Her eyes bleed tears, His wounds weep blood.

[1] The Cross.
[2] His own eyes, which should be weeping.

III

O costly intercourse
Of deaths, and worse—
Divided loves.   While Son and mother
Discourse alternate wounds to one another,
    Quick deaths that grow
    And gather, as they come and go.
His nails write swords in her, which soon her heart
    Pays back, with more than their own smart ;
Her swords, still growing with His pain,
Turn spears, and straight come home again.

IV

She sees her Son, her God,
    Bow with a load
    Of borrow'd sins ; and swim
In woes that were not made for Him.
    Ah, hard command
    Of love !   Here must she stand,
Charged to look on, and with a steadfast eye
    See her life [1] die ;
Leaving her only so much breath
As serves to keep alive her death.

V

O mother turtle-dove !
    Soft source of love !
    That these dry lids might borrow
Something from thy full seas of sorrow !
    O in that breast
    Of thine (the noblest nest

[1] Him that was the life of Her.

Both of Love's fires and floods) might I recline
  This hard, cold heart of mine !
The chill lump would relent, and prove
Soft subject for the siege of Love.

VI

  O teach those wounds to bleed
  In me ; me, so to read
  This book of loves, thus writ
In lines of death, my life may copy it
  With loyal cares.
  O let me, here, claim shares,
Yield something in thy sad prerogative
  (Great Queen of griefs !), and give
Me too, my tears ; who, though all stone,
Think much that thou shouldst mourn alone.

VII

  Yea, let my life and me
  Fix here with thee,
  And at the humble foot
Of this fair tree,[1] take our eternal root.
  That so we may
  At least be in Love's way ;
And in these chaste wars, while the wing'd wounds
  flee
  So fast 'twixt Him and Thee,
My breast may catch the kiss of some kind dart,
Though as at second hand, from either heart.

     [1] The Cross.

VIII

O you, your own best darts,
Dear, doleful hearts ;
Hail ! and strike home, and make me see
That wounded bosoms their own weapons be.
Come wounds, come darts !
Nail'd hands and piercèd hearts !
Come your whole selves, Sorrow's great Son and
Mother !
Nor grudge a younger brother
Of griefs his portion, who (had all their due)
One single wound should not have left for you.

IX

Shall I set there in sins
So deep a share,
(Dear wounds !), and only now
In sorrows draw no dividend with you?
O be more wise,
If not more soft, mine eyes !
Flow, tardy founts ! and into decent showers
Dissolve my days and hours.
And if thou yet (faint soul !) defer
To bleed with Him, fail not to weep with her.

X

Rich queen, lend some relief ;
At least an alms of grief,
To a heart who by sad right of sin
Could prove the whole sum (too sure) due to him.

2

By all those stings
Of Love, sweet-bitter things,
Which these torn hands transcribed on thy true
heart ;
O teach mine, too, the art
To study Him so, till we mix
Wounds, and become one crucifix.

XI

Oh, let me suck the wine
So long of this chaste Vine,
Till drunk of the dear wounds, I be
A lost thing to the world, as it to me.
O faithful friend
Of me and of my end ;
Fold up my life in love ; and lay't beneath
My dear Lord's vital death.
Lo, heart, thy hope's whole plea ! her precious
breath
Pour'd out in prayers for thee ; thy Lord's in death.

THE TEAR

I

WHAT bright soft thing is this,
Sweet Mary, thy fair eyes' expense ?
A moist spark it is,
A watery diamond, from whence
The very tearme,[1] I think, was found,
The water of a diamond.

[1] Term.

II

O, 'tis not a tear,
  'Tis a star about to drop
From thine eye, its sphere ;
  The Sun will stoop and take it up.
Proud will his sister be to wear
This thine eye's jewel in her ear.

III

O, 'tis a tear,
  Too true a tear ; for no sad eyne,[1]
How sad soe'er,
  Rain so true a tear as thine ;
Each drop, leaving a place so dear,
Weeps for itself, is its own tear.

IV

Such a pearl as this is,
  (Slipp'd from Aurora's [2] dewy breast)
The rosebud's sweet lip kisses ;
  And such the rose itself, that's vex'd
With ungentle flames, does shed,
Sweating in a too warm bed.[3]

V

Such the maiden gem
  By the purpling vine put on,

[1] Eyes.   [2] Greek Eos (Ἠώς), the goddess of dawn.
[3] Stanza iv. has two lines from stanza xxix. of " The Weeper."

Peeps from her parent stem,
    And blushes on the bridegroom Sun:
The watery blossom of thy eyne,
Ripe, will make the richer wine.

VI

Fair drop, why quak'st thou so?
    'Cause thou straight must lay thy head
In the dust?   O no;
    The dust shall never be thy bed:
A pillow for thee will I bring,
Stuffed with down of angel's wing.

VII

Thus carried up on high,
    (For to Heaven thou must go)
Sweetly shalt thou lie,
    And in soft slumbers bathe thy woe;
Till the singing orbs[1] awake thee,
And one of their bright chorus make thee.

VIII

There thyself shalt be
    An eye, but not a weeping one;
Yet I doubt of thee,
    Whether th' had'st rather there have
        shone
An eye of Heaven; or still shine here
In the Heaven of Mary's eye, a TEAR.

[1] Stars.

THE OFFICE OF THE HOLY CROSS

Tradidit semetipsum pro nobis oblationem et hostiam Deo in odorem suavitatis.—*Ad Eph*. v. 2.

THE HOURS

FOR THE HOUR OF MATINS [1]

The Versicle

LORD, by Thy sweet and saving sign,[2]

The Responsory

Defend us from our foes and Thine.

V. Thou shalt open my lips, O Lord,

R. And my mouth shall shew forth Thy praise.

V. O God, make speed to save me.

R. O Lord, make haste to help me.

V. Glory be to the Father,
    and to the Son,
    and to the Holy Ghost.

R. As it was in the beginning, is now, and ever
    shall be, world without end. Amen.

---

[1] The "Hours" were usually said as follows:—
  Matins, between nine at night and dawn.
  Prime, at six o'clock, morning.
  Tierce, or the Third, at nine morning.
  Sext, or the Sixth, at noon.
  Nones, or the Ninth, at three afternoon.
  Evensong, at six evening.
  Compline, at nine evening,
but there was no rule.
  [2] The Cross.

The Hymn

The wakeful Matins haste to sing
The unknown sorrows of our King:
The Father's Word and Wisdom, made
Man for man, by man's betray'd;
The World's Price set to sale, and by the bold
Merchants of Death and Sin, is bought and sold:
Of His best friends (yea of Himself) forsaken;
By His worst foes (because He would) besieged
    and taken.

The Antiphon

All hail, fair Tree
Whose fruit we be;
What song shall raise
Thy seemly praise,
Who brought'st to light
Life out of Death, Day out of Night?

The Versicle

Lo, we adore Thee,
Dread Lamb, and bow thus low before Thee.

The Responsory

'Cause by the covenant of Thy Cross
Thou hast saved at once the whole World's loss.

The Prayer

O Lord Jesu Christ, Son of the living God,
interpose, I pray Thee, Thine Own precious Death,
Thy Cross and Passion, betwixt my soul and Thy
Judgment, now and in the hour of my death. And

vouchsafe to grant unto me Thy grace and mercy; unto all quick and dead, remission and rest; to Thy Church, peace and concord; to us sinners, life and glory everlasting. Who livest and reignest with the Father, in the unity of the Holy Ghost, one God, world without end. Amen.

FOR THE HOUR OF PRIME

The Versicle

LORD, by Thy sweet and saving Sign,

The Responsory

Defend us from our foes and Thine.

V. Thou shalt open my lips, O Lord,

R. And my mouth shall shew forth Thy praise.

V. O God, make speed to save me.

R. O Lord, make haste to help me.

V. Glory be, etc.

R. As it was, etc.

THE HYMN

The early Prime blushes to say
She could not rise so soon, as they
Call'd Pilate up, to try if he
Could lend them any cruelty;
Their hands with lashes arm'd, their tongues with
  lies,
And loathsome spittle, blot those beauteous eyes,
The blissful springs of joy; from whose all-
  cheering ray
The fair stars fill their wakeful fires, the sun him-
  self drinks day.

The Antiphon

Victorious Sign
That now dost shine,
Transcribed above
Into the land of light and love ;
O let us twine
Our roots with Thine,
That we may rise
Upon Thy wings and reach the skies.

The Versicle

Lo, we adore Thee,
Dread Lamb, and fall
Thus low before Thee.

The Responsory

'Cause by the covenant of Thy Cross
Thou hast saved at once the whole World's loss.

The Prayer

O Lord JESU CHRIST, Son of the living God,
interpose, I pray Thee, Thine Own precious Death,
Thy Cross and Passion, betwixt my soul and Thy
Judgment, now and in the hour of my death. And
vouchsafe to grant unto me Thy grace and mercy ;
unto all quick and dead, remission and rest; to
Thy Church, peace and concord; to us sinners,
life and glory everlasting. Who livest and reignest
with the Father, in the unity of the Holy Ghost,
one God, world without end. Amen.

THE THIRD

The Versicle

LORD, by Thy sweet and saving Sign,

The Responsory

Defend us from our foes and Thine.
V. Thou shalt open my lips, O Lord,
R. And my mouth shall shew forth Thy praise.
V. O God, make speed to save me.
R. O Lord, make haste to help me.
V. Glory be to, etc.
R. As it was in the, etc.

THE HYMN

The third hour's deafen'd with the cry
Of "Crucify Him, crucify."
So goes the vote (nor ask them, why?)
"Live Barabbas! and let God die."
But there is wit in wrath, and they will try
A "Hail" more cruel than their "Crucify."
For while in sport He wears a spiteful crown,
The serious showers along His decent Face run
    sadly down.

The Antiphon

Christ when He died
Deceived the Cross;
And on Death's side
Threw all the loss.
The captive World awaked and found
The prisoners loose, the jailer bound.

The Versicle

Lo, we adore Thee,
Dread Lamb, and fall
Thus low before Thee.

The Responsory

'Cause by the covenant of Thy Cross
Thou hast saved at once the whole World's loss.

The Prayer

O Lord JESU CHRIST, Son of the living God,
interpose, I pray Thee, Thine Own precious
Death, Thy Cross and Passion, betwixt my soul and
Thy Judgment, now and in the hour of my death.
And vouchsafe to grant unto me Thy grace and
mercy; unto all quick and dead, remission and
rest; to Thy Church, peace and concord; to us
sinners, life and glory everlasting. Who livest
and reignest with the Father, in the unity of the
Holy Ghost, one God, world without end.
Amen.

THE SIXTH

The Versicle

LORD, by Thy sweet and saving Sign,

The Responsory

Defend us from our foes and Thine.
V. Thou shalt open my lips, O Lord,
R And my mouth shall shew forth Thy praise.

V. O God, make speed to save me.
R. O Lord, make haste to help me.
V. Glory be, etc.
R. As it was, etc.

The Hymn

Now is the noon of Sorrows night:
High in His patience, as their spite,
Lo, the faint Lamb, with weary limb,
Bears that huge tree which must bear Him.
The fatal plant, so great of fame,
For fruit of sorrow and of shame,
Shall swell with both, for Him, and mix
All woes into one crucifix.
Is tortured thirst itself too sweet a cup?
Gall, and more bitter mocks, shall make it up.
Are nails blunt pens of superficial smart?
Contempt and scorn can send sure wounds to search
    the inmost heart.

The Antiphon

O dear and sweet dispute
'Twixt Death's and Love's far different fruit!
Different as far
As antidotes and poisons are
By that first fatal tree [1]
Both life and liberty
Were sold and slain;
By this they both look up, and live again.

[1] The tree of knowledge in the Garden of Eden.

The Versicle

Lo, we adore Thee,
Dread Lamb, and bow thus low before Thee.

The Responsory

'Cause by the covenant of Thy Cross,
Thou hast saved at once the whole World's loss.

The Prayer

O Lord JESU CHRIST, Son of the living God,
interpose, I pray Thee, Thine Own precious
Death, Thy Cross and Passion, betwixt my soul
and Thy Judgment, now and in the hour of my
death. And vouchsafe to grant unto me Thy
grace and mercy; unto all quick and dead, remis-
sion and rest; to Thy Church, peace and concord;
to us sinners, life and glory everlasting. Who livest
and reignest with the Father, in the unity of the
Holy Ghost, one God, world without end. Amen.

THE NINTH

The Versicle

LORD, by Thy sweet and saving Sign,

The Responsory

Defend us from our foes and Thine.
V. Thou shalt open my lips, O Lord,
R. And my mouth shall shew forth Thy praise.
V. O God, make speed to save me.
R. O Lord, make haste to help me.
V. Glory, etc.
R. As it was, etc.

The Hymn

The Ninth with awful horror hearkened to those
    groans
Which taught attention even to rocks and stones.
Hear, Father, hear! Thy Lamb (at last) com-
    plains
Of some more painful thing than all His pains.
Then bows His all-obedient head, and dies,
His own love's, and our sins' great Sacrifice.
The sun saw that, and would have seen no more ;
The centre shook : her useless veil th' inglorious
    Temple tore.

The Antiphon

O strange, mysterious strife
Of open Death and hidden Life !
When on the Cross my King did bleed,
Life seem'd to die, Death died indeed.

The Versicle

Lo, we adore Thee,
Dread Lamb, and fall
Thus low before Thee.

The Responsory

'Cause by the covenant of Thy cross
Thou hast saved at once the whole World's loss.

The Prayer

O Lord Jesu Christ, Son of the living God,
interpose, I pray Thee, Thine Own precious Death,
Thy Cross and Passion, betwixt my soul and Thy

Judgment, now and in the hour of my death.   And
vouchsafe to grant unto me Thy grace and mercy;
unto all quick and dead, remission and rest; to Thy
Church, peace and concord; to us sinners, life and
glory everlasting.   Who livest and reignest with the
Father, in the unity of the Holy Ghost, one God,
world without end.   Amen.

EVENSONG

The Versicle

LORD, by Thy sweet and saving Sign,

The Responsory

Defend us from our foes and Thine.
V. Thou shalt open my lips, O Lord,
R. And my mouth shall shew forth Thy praise.
V. O God, make speed to save me.
R. O Lord, make haste to help me.
V. Glory, etc.
R. As it was, etc.

THE HYMN

But there were rocks [1] would not relent at this:
Lo, for their own hearts, they rend His;
Their deadly hate lives still, and hath
A wild reserve of wanton wrath;
Superfluous spear! but there's a heart stands by
Will look no wounds be lost, no Death shall die.
Gather now thy grief's ripe fruit, great Mother-maid,
Then sit thee down, and sing thine evensong in
    the sad Tree's shade.

[1] The hearts of those who crucified Him.

The Antiphon

O sad, sweet Tree,
Woeful and joyful we
Both weep and sing in shade of thee.
When the dear nails did lock
And graft into thy gracious stock
The hope, the health,
The worth, the wealth
Of all the ransomed World, Thou hadst the power
(In that propitious hour)
To poise each precious limb,
And prove how light the World was, when it
weighed with Him.
Wide mayest thou spread
Thine arms, and with Thy bright and blissful head
O'erlook all Libanus.[1]   Thy lofty crown
The King Himself is, thou His humble throne,
Where yielding and yet conquering He
Proved a new path of patient victory:
When wondering Death by death was slain,
And our Captivity His captive ta'en.

The Versicle

Lo, we adore Thee,
Dread Lamb, and bow thus low before Thee.

The Responsory

'Cause by the covenant of Thy cross
Thou hast saved at once the whole World's loss.

[1] The mountains of Libanus are to the extreme north
of Palestine, and famous for cedars. This probably
means that the Cross having borne our Saviour is greater
than all other trees.

The Prayer

O Lord Jesu Christ, Son of the living God, etc.

COMPLINE

The Versicle

Lord, by Thy sweet and saving Sign,

The Responsory

Defend us from our foes and Thine.

V. Thou shalt open my lips, O Lord,

R. And my mouth shall shew forth Thy praise.

V. O God, make speed to save me.

R. O Lord, make haste to help me.

V. Glory be, etc.

R. As it was, etc.

THE HYMN

The Compline hour comes last, to call
Us to our own lives' funeral.
Ah, heartless task! yet Hope takes head,
And lives in Him that here lies dead.
Run, Mary, run! bring hither all the blest
Arabia,[1] for thy Royal Phœnix' nest;
Pour on thy noblest sweets, which, when they touch
This sweeter Body, shall indeed be such.
But must Thy bed, Lord, be a borrowed grave,
Who lend'st to all things all the life they have?
O rather use this heart, thus far a fitter stone,
'Cause, though a hard and cold one, yet it is Thine
    own.   Amen.

[1] Cf. "All the perfumes of Arabia "—*Macbeth*; and
John xii. 3.

The Antiphon

O save us then,
Merciful King of men !
Since Thou wouldst needs be thus
A Saviour, and at such a rate,[1] for us ;
Save us, O save us, Lord.
We now will own no shorter wish, nor name a
narrower word ;
Thy Blood bids us be bold,
Thy Wounds give us fair hold,
Thy Sorrows chide our shame :
Thy Cross, Thy Nature, and Thy Name
Advance our claim,
And cry with one accord,
Save them, O save them, Lord !

THE RECOMMENDATION

These Hours, and that which hovers o'er my end,
Into Thy hands and heart, Lord, I commend.

Take both to Thine account, that I and mine,
In that hour and in these, may be all Thine.

That as I dedicate my devoutest breath
To make a kind of life for my Lord's death,

So from His living, and life-giving death,
My dying life may draw a new and never fleeting
breath.

[1] Terrible payment, price.

3

VEXILLA REGIS

I

LOOK up, languishing soul! Lo, where the fair
  Badge of thy Faith calls back thy care,
    And bids thee ne'er forget
    Thy life is one long debt
Of love to Him, Who on this painful Tree [1]
Paid back the flesh He took for thee.

II

Lo, how the streams of life, from that full nest,
Of loves, Thy Lord's too liberal breast,
    Flow in an amorous flood
    Of water wedding blood.
With these He wash'd thy stain, transferr'd thy
    smart,
And took it home to His own Heart.

III

But though great Love, greedy of such sad gain,
Usurp'd the portion of thy pain,
    And from the nails and spear
    Turn'd the steel point of fear:
Their use is changed, not lost; and now they
    move
Not stings of wrath, but wounds of love.

[1] Cross.

IV

Tall Tree of life ! thy truth makes good
What was till now ne'er understood,
   Though the prophetic king
   Struck loud his faithful string :
It was thy wood he meant should make the throne
For a more than Solomon.

V

Large throne of Love, royally spread
With purple of too rich a red,
   Thy crime is too much duty,
   Thy burthen too much beauty.
Glorious or grievous more ? thus to make good
Thy costly excellence with thy King's own blood.

VI

Even balance of both worlds ; our world of sin,
And that of grace, Heaven weighed in Him :
   Us with our price thou weighedst ;
   Our price for us thou payedst,
Soon as the right-hand scale rejoiced to prove
How much Death weigh'd more light than Love.

VII

Hail, our alone hope ! let thy fair head shoot
Aloft, and fill the nations with thy noble fruit :
   The while our hearts and we
   Thus graft ourselves on thee,
Grow thou and they. And be thy fair increase
The sinner's pardon and the just man's peace.

Live, O for ever live and reign
The Lamb Whom His own love hath slain ;
And let Thy lost sheep live to inherit
That kingdom which this Holy Cross did merit.
                                        Amen.

NO MAN WAS ABLE TO ANSWER HIM

NEITHER DURST ANY MAN FROM THAT DAY ASK HIM
ANY MORE QUESTIONS.—MATT. xxii. 46.

MIDST all the dark and knotty snares,
    Black wit or malice can or dares,
Thy glorious wisdom breaks the nets,
And treads with uncontrollèd steps.
Thy quell'd foes are not only now
Thy triumphs, but Thy trophies too.
They both at once Thy conquests be,
And Thy conquests' memory.
Stony amazement makes them stand
Waiting on Thy victorious hand,
Like statues fixèd to the fame
Of Thy renown, and their own shame,
As if they only meant to breathe,
To be the life of their own death.
'Twas time to hold their peace when they
Had ne'er another word to say :
Yet is their silence, unto Thee
The full sound of Thy victory ;
Their silence speaks aloud, and is
Thy well pronounc'd panegyris.[1]
While they speak nothing, they speak all
Their share in Thy memorial.

[1] Praise.

While they speak nothing, they proclaim
Thee with the shrillest trump of fame.
To hold their peace is all the ways
These wretches have to speak Thy praise.

ON THE WOUNDS OF OUR CRUCIFIED LORD

O THESE wakeful wounds of Thine!
   Are they mouths? or are they eyes?
Be they mouths, or be they eyne,[1]
   Each bleeding part some one supplies.

Lo! a mouth, whose full-bloom'd lips
   At too dear a rate are roses:
Lo! a blood-shot eye that weeps,
   And many a cruel tear discloses.

O Thou,[2] that on this foot hast laid
   Many a kiss, and many a tear;
Now thou shalt have all repaid,
   Whatsoe'er thy charges were.

This foot hath got a mouth and lips,
   To pay the sweet sum of thy kisses;
To pay thy tears, an eye that weeps,
   Instead of tears, such gems as this is.

The difference only this appears,
   (Nor can the change offend)
The debt is paid in ruby tears,
   Which thou in pearls didst lend. .

[1] Eyes.   [2] Possibly St. Mary Magdalene.

UPON THE BLEEDING CRUCIFIX

A SONG

I

JESU, no more!   It is full tide ;
  From Thy hands and from Thy feet,
From Thy head, and from Thy side,
  All the purple rivers meet.

II

What need Thy fair head bear a part
  In showers, as if Thine eyes had none ?
What need they help to drown Thy heart,
  That strives in torrents of its own ?

III

Water'd by the showers they bring,
  The thorns that Thy blest brow encloses
(A cruel and a costly spring)
  Conceive proud hopes of proving roses.

IV

Thy restless feet now cannot go
  For us and our eternal good,
As they were ever wont.   What though ?[1]
  They swim, alas ! in their own flood.
    [1] What though they cannot ?

v

Thy hand to give Thou canst not lift,
    Yet will Thy hand still giving be.
It gives, but O itself's the gift,
    It gives though bound, though bound 'tis free.

vi

But, O Thy side, Thy deep-digg'd side,
    That hath a double Nilus going :
Nor ever was the Pharoan tide
    Half so fruitful, half so flowing.

vii

No hair so small, but pays his river
    To this Red Sea of Thy blood ;
Their little channels can deliver
    Something to the general flood.

viii

But while I speak, whither are run
    All the rivers named before?
I counted wrong : there is but one ;
    But O that one is one all o'er.

ix

Rain-swol'n rivers may rise proud,
    Bent all to drown and overflow ;
But when indeed all's overflow'd,
    They themselves are drownèd too.

x

This Thy blood's deluge (a dire chance,
    Dear Lord, to Thee) to us is found
A deluge of deliverance;
    A deluge lest we should be drown'd.
        Ne'er wast Thou in a sense so sadly true,
        The well of living waters, Lord, till now.

TO THE NAME ABOVE EVERY NAME, THE NAME OF JESUS

A HYMN

I SING the Name which none can say
    But touch'd with an interior ray:
The Name of our new peace, our good,
Our bliss, and supernatural blood.
The Name of all our lives and loves;
Hearken, and help, ye holy doves,
The high-born brood of Day, you bright
Candidates of blissful light,
The heirs elect of Love, whose names belong
Unto the everlasting life of song.
All ye wise souls, who in the wealthy breast
Of this unbounded Name, build your warm nest.
Awake, my glory, Soul, (if such thou be,
And that fair word at all refer to thee),
        Awake and sing,
        And be all wing;
Bring hither thy whole self, and let me see
What of thy parent Heaven yet speaks in thee.

O thou art poor of noble powers, I see,
And full of nothing else but empty me ;
Narrow, and low, and infinitely less
Than this great morning's mighty business.
     One little world or two
     (Alas !) will never do,
     We must have store ;
Go, Soul, out of thyself, and seek for more.
     Go and request
Great Nature for the key of her huge chest
Of Heavens, the self-involving set of spheres
(Which dull mortality more feels than hears).
     Then rouse the nest
Of nimble Art, and traverse round
The airy shop of soul-appeasing sound :
And beat a summons in the same
     All-sovereign Name,
To warn each several kind
And shape of sweetness, be they such
     As sigh with subtle wind
     Or answer artful touch ;
That they convene and come away
To wait at the love-crowned doors of this illustrious
     day.
Shall we dare this, my Soul ? we'll do 't and bring
No other note for 't, but the Name we sing.
Wake lute and harp, and every sweet-lipped thing
     That talks with tuneful string ;
Start into life, and leap with me
Into a hasty fit-tuned harmony.
     Nor must you think it much
     T' obey my bolder touch ;
I have authority in Love's name to take you,
And to the work of Love this morning wake you.

Wake, in the Name
Of Him Who never sleeps, all things that are,
  Or, what's the same,
  Are musical;
  Answer my call
  And come along;
Help me to meditate mine immortal song.
Come, ye soft ministers of sweet sad mirth,
Bring all your household-stuff of Heaven on earth;
O you, my Soul's most certain wings,
Complaining pipes, and prattling strings,
  Bring all the store
Of sweets you have; and murmur that you have no
    more.
  Come, ne'er to part,
  Nature and Art.
  Come, and come strong,
To the conspiracy of our spacious song.
  Bring all the powers of praise,
Your provinces of well-united worlds can raise;
Bring all your lutes and harps of Heaven and
  Earth,
Whate'er co-operates to the common mirth;
  Vessels of vocal joys,
Or you, more noble architects of intellectual noise,
Cymbals of Heaven, or human spheres,
Solicitors [1] of souls or ears;
  And when you are come, with all
That you can bring or we can call:
  O may you fix
  For ever here, and mix
  Yourselves into the long
And everlasting series of a deathless song;

[1] Petitioners; the word is so used by Addison.

Mix all your many worlds above,[1]
And loose them into one of love.
    Cheer thee my heart!
    For thou too hast thy part
    And place in the great throng
Of this unbounded all-embracing song.
    Powers of my soul, be proud,
    And speak ye loud
To all the dear-bought Nations this redeeming
    Name,
And in the wealth of one rich word, proclaim
New similes to Nature.   May it be no wrong,
Blest Heavens, to you and your superior song,
That we, dark sons of dust and sorrow,
    A while dare borrow
The name of your delights, and our desires,
And fit it to so far inferior lyres.
Our murmurs have their music too,
Ye mighty Orbs, as well as you;
    Nor yields the noblest nest
Of warbling Seraphim to the ears of Love,
A choicer lesson than the joyful breast
    Of a poor panting turtle-dove.
And we, low worms, have leave to do
The same bright business (ye Third Heavens) with
    you.
Gentle spirits, do not complain,
    We will have care
    To keep it fair,
And send it back to you again.
Come, lovely Name, appear from forth the bright
    Regions of peaceful light;

[1] Possibly referring to the Seven Heavens.   See below,
where he mentions the Third Heaven.

Look from Thine Own illustrious home,
Fair King of names, and come ;
Leave all Thy native glories in their gorgeous
    nest
And give Thy Self a while the gracious Guest
Of humble souls, that seek to find
      The hidden sweets
      Which man's heart meets
When Thou art Master of the mind.
Come, lovely Name ; Life of our hope,
Lo, we hold our hearts wide ope ;
Unlock Thy cabinet of Day,
Dearest Sweet, and come away.
      Lo, how the thirsty lands
Gasp for Thy golden showers ! with long-stretch'd
    hands.
      Lo, how the labouring Earth
      That hopes to be
      All Heaven by Thee,
      Leaps at Thy birth !
The attending World, to wait Thy rise,
      First turn'd to eyes ;
And then, not knowing what to do,
Turn'd them to tears, and spent them too.
Come, royal Name, and pay the expense
Of all this precious patience ;
      O come away
And kill the death of this delay.
O see so many worlds of barren years
Melted and measured out in seas of tears ;
O see the weary lids of wakeful Hope
(Love's eastern windows) all wide ope
      With curtains drawn,
To catch the daybreak of Thy dawn.

O dawn at last, long-look'd for Day,
Take Thine own wings and come away.
Lo, where aloft it comes !   It comes, among
The conduct [1] of adoring spirits, that throng
Like diligent bees, and swarm about it.
   O they are wise,
And know what sweets are suck'd from out it :
   It is the hive,
   By which they thrive,
Where all their hoard of honey lies.
Lo, where it comes, upon the snowy Dove's
Soft back ; and brings a bosom big with loves ;
Welcome to our dark world, Thou womb of Day !
Unfold Thy fair conceptions, and display
The birth of our bright joys, O Thou compacted
Body of blessings, Spirit of souls extracted.
O dissipate Thy spicy powers,
(Cloud of condensèd sweets) and break upon us
   In balmy showers.
O fill our senses, and take from us
All force of so profane a fallacy,
To think ought sweet but that which smells of
  Thee !
Fair, flowery Name, in none but Thee
And Thy nectareal fragrancy,
   Hourly there meets
An universal synod of all sweets ;
By whom it is definèd thus,
   That no perfume
   For ever shall presume
To pass for odoriferous,
But such alone whose sacred pedigree
Can prove itself some kin (sweet Name) to Thee.
    [1] The train, the retinue.

Sweet Name, in Thy each syllable
A thousand blest Arabias [1] dwell;
A thousand hills of frankincense;
Mountains of myrrh, and beds of spices
And ten thousand Paradises,
The soul that tastes Thee takes from thence.
How many unknown worlds there are
Of comforts, which Thou hast been keeping!
How many thousand mercies there
In Pity's soft lap lie a-sleeping!
Happy he who has the art
    To awake them,
    And to take them
Home, and lodge them in his heart.
O that it were as it was wont to be,
When Thy old friends [2] of fire, all full of Thee,
Fought against frowns with smiles; gave glorious
    chase
To persecutions; and against the face
Of Death and fiercest dangers, durst with brave
And sober pace, march on to meet A GRAVE
On their bold breasts, about the world they bore
    Thee,
And to the teeth of Hell stood up to teach [3] Thee,
    In centre of their inmost souls, they wore
      Thee;
Where racks and torments strove, in vain, to reach
    Thee.
    Little, alas thought they
Who tore the fair breasts of Thy friends,
    Their fury but made way
For Thee, and served them in Thy glorious ends.

[1] Cf. *Macbeth*, v. 1; and *Cymbeline*, i. 6.
[2] The saints.   [3] To teach the world about Thee.

What did their weapons but with wider pores
Enlarge Thy flaming-breasted lovers,
    More.freely to transpire
    That impatient fire,
The heart that hides Thee hardly covers?
What did their weapons but set wide the doors
For Thee? fair, purple doors, of Love's devising;
The ruby windows which enrich'd the East
Of Thy so oft-repeated rising;
Each wound of theirs was Thy new morning,
And re-enthroned Thee in Thy rosy nest,
With blush of Thine Own blood Thy day adorning:
It was the wit of Love o'erflow'd the bounds
Of Wrath, and made Thee way through all those
    wounds.
Welcome, dear, all-adorèd Name!
    For sure there is no knee
    That knows not Thee:
Or, if there be such sons of shame,
    Alas! what will they do
When stubborn rocks shall bow,
And hills hang down their heaven-saluting heads
    To seek for humble beds
Of dust, where in the bashful shades of Night,
Next to their own low Nothing, they may lie,
And couch before the dazzling light of Thy dread
    majesty.
They that by Love's mild dictate now
    Will not adore Thee,
Shall then, with just confusion bow
    And break before Thee.

PSALM XXIII

HAPPY me, O happy sheep,
　　Whom my God vouchsafes to
　　　keep;
Even my God, even He it is
That points me to these ways of bliss;
On Whose pastures cheerful Spring
All the year doth sit and sing,
And rejoicing, smiles to see
Their green backs wear His livery.
Pleasure sings my soul to rest,
Plenty wears me at her breast,
Whose sweet temper teaches me
Nor wanton, nor in want to be.
At my feet the blubbering mountain
Weeping, melts into a fountain,
Whose soft, silver-sweating streams
Make high-noon forget his beams:
When my wayward breath is flying,
He calls home my soul from dying,
Strokes and tames my rabid grief,
And does woo me into life:
When my simple weakness strays,
(Tangled in forbidden ways)
He (my Shepherd) is my guide,
He's before me, at my side,
And behind me; He beguiles
Craft in all her knotty wiles.
He expounds the weary wonder
Of my giddy steps, and under

Spreads a path clear as the day,
Where no churlish rub[1] says nay
To my joy-conducted feet,
Whilst they gladly go to meet
Grace and Peace, to learn new lays
Tuned to my great Shepherd's praise.
Come now, all ye terrors sally,
Muster forth into the valley,
Where triumphant darkness hovers
With a sable wing, that covers
Brooding horror.   Come, thou Death,
Let the damps of thy dull breath
Overshadow even the shade,
And make Darkness' self afraid ;
There my feet, even there, shall find
Way for a resolvèd mind.
Still my Shepherd, still my God
Thou art with me ; still Thy rod,
And Thy staff, whose influence
Gives direction, gives defence.
At the whisper of Thy word
Crown'd abundance spreads my board :
While I feast, my foes do feed
Their rank malice, not their need ;
So that with the self-same bread
They are starved, and I am fed.
How my head in ointment swims,
How my cup o'erlooks her brims ;
So, even so, still may I move
By the line of Thy dear love ;

[1] A difficulty. Cf. *Macbeth*, iii. 1 ; *Henry V.*, ii. 2 ;
and *Hamlet*, iii. 1—

> " To sleep, perchance to dream,
>   Ay, there's the rub."

4

Still may Thy sweet mercy spread
A shady arm above my head,
About my paths; so shall I find
The fair centre of my mind,
Thy temple, and those lovely walls
Bright ever with a beam that falls
Fresh from th' pure glance of Thine eye,
Lighting to Eternity.
There I'll dwell for ever, there
Will I find a purer air,
To feed my life with; there I'll sup
Balm and nectar in my cup;
And thence my ripe soul will I breathe
Warm into the arms of Death.

PSALM CXXXVII

ON the proud banks of great Euphrates' flood,
  There we sate, and there we wept:
Our harps, that now no music understood,
  Nodding, on the willows slept:
    While unhappy captived we,
    Lovely Sion, thought on thee.
They, they that snatch'd us from our country's
    breast
  Would have a song carved [1] to their ears
In Hebrew numbers, then (O cruel jest)
  When harps and hearts were drown'd in tears:
    Come, they cried, come sing and play
    One of Sion's songs to-day.

[1] Carved as it were from absolute melody.   Made for
them especially.

Sing? play? to whom (ah!) shall we sing or play,
  If not, Jerusalem, to thee?
Ah! thee Jerusalem, ah! sooner may
    This hand forget the mastery
      Of Music's dainty touch, than I
      The music of thy memory.
Which, when I lose, O may at once my tongue
  Lose this same busy-speaking art;
Unperched,[1] her vocal arteries unstrung,
    No more acquainted with my heart,
      On my dry palate's roof to rest
      A withered leaf, an idle guest.
No, no, Thy good, Sion, alone must crown
  The head of all thy hope-nursed joys.
But Edom, cruel thou, thou criedst down, down
    Sink Sion, down and never rise;
      Her falling thou didst urge and thrust,
      And haste to dash her into dust:
Dost laugh proud Babel's[2] daughter? do, laugh on,
  Till thy ruin teach thee tears,
Even such as these; laugh, till a 'venging throng
    Of woes too late do rouse thy fears:
      Laugh till thy children's bleeding bones
      Weep precious tears upon the stones.

[1] An extraordinary use of the word, but see following line. The idea is that the tongue is perched on the palate to sing.

[2] Babylon's daughter.

IN THE HOLY NATIVITY OF OUR LORD GOD

A HYMN SUNG AS BY THE SHEPHERDS

THE HYMN

Chorus

COME, ye shepherds, whose blest sight
    Hath met Love's noon in Nature's night;
Come, lift we up our loftier song,
And wake the sun that lies too long.

To all our world of well-stolen joy
He[1] slept, and dreamt of no such thing.
    While we found out Heaven's fairer eye,
And kissed the cradle of our King.
    Tell Him he rises now, too late
To·show us aught worth looking at.

    Tell him we now can show him more
Than he e'er show'd to mortal sight;
    Than he himself e'er saw before,
Which to be seen needs not his light.
    Tell him, Tityrus, where th' hast been,
Tell him, Thyrsis, what th' hast seen.

Tityrus

Gloomy night embraced the place
Where the noble Infant lay.

[1] The Sun.

The Babe looked up and showed His face;
In spite of darkness, it was day.
It was Thy day, Sweet, and did rise,
Not from the East, but from Thine eyes.

Chorus

It was Thy day, Sweet . . .

Thyrsis

Winter chid aloud, and sent
The angry North to wage his wars.
The North forgot his fierce intent,
· And left perfumes instead of scars.
By those sweet eyes' persuasive powers,
Where he meant frost, he scattered flowers.

Chorus

By those sweet eyes' . . .

Both

We saw Thee in Thy balmy nest,
Young dawn of our eternal Day;
We saw Thine eyes break from their East,
And chase the trembling shades away.
We saw Thee, and we blest the sight,
We saw Thee by Thine Own sweet light.

Tityrus

Poor world (said I), what wilt thou do
To entertain this starry Stranger?
Is this the best thou canst bestow,
A cold, and not too cleanly, manger?
Contend, the powers of Heaven and Earth,
To fit a bed for this huge birth?

Chorus

Contend, the powers . . .

Thyrsis

Proud world, said I, cease your contest,
And let the mighty Babe alone.
The phœnix builds the phœnix' nest,
Love's architecture is his own.
The Babe whose birth embraves [1] this morn,
Made His Own bed ere He was born.

Chorus

The Babe whose . . .

Tityrus

I saw the curled drops, soft and slow,
Come hovering o'er the place's head ;
Offering their whitest sheets of snow
To furnish the fair Infant's bed :
Forbear, said I ; be not too bold,
Your fleece is white, but 'tis too cold.

Chorus

Forbear, said I . . .

Thyrsis

I saw the obsequious [2] Seraphim
Their rosy fleece of fire bestow,

[1] Decorates, and so honours.
[2] Obedient, willing.

For well they now can spare their wing,
Since Heaven itself lies here below.
  Well done, said I, but are you sure
Your down so warm, will pass for pure?

Chorus

Well done, said I . . .

Tityrus

No, no, your King's not yet to seek
Where to repose His royal head;
  See, see, how soon His new-bloom'd cheek
'Twixt's Mother's breasts is gone to bed.
  Sweet choice, said we, no way but so
Not to lie cold, yet sleep in snow.

Chorus

Sweet choice, said we . . .

Both

We saw Thee in Thy balmy nest,
Bright dawn of our eternal Day!
  We saw Thine eyes break from their East,
And chase the trembling shades away.
  We saw Thee, and we blest the sight,
We saw Thee by Thine Own sweet light.

Chorus

We saw Thee . . .

Full Chorus

Welcome, all wonders in one sight,
Eternity shut in a span,
   Summer in Winter, Day in Night,
Heaven in Earth, and God in man,
   Great, little One, whose all-embracing birth
Lifts Earth to Heaven, stoops Heaven to Earth.

   Welcome, though not to gold nor silk,
To more than Cæsar's birthright is,
   Two sister-seas of virgin-milk,
With many a rarely-tempered kiss,
   That breathes at once both maid and mother,
Warms in the one, cools in the other.

   She sings Thy tears asleep, and dips
Her kisses in Thy weeping eye ;
   She spreads the red leaves of Thy lips,
That in their buds yet blushing lie :
   She 'gainst those mother-diamonds, tries
The points of Her young eagle's eyes.

   Welcome, though not to those gay flies,[1]
Gilded i' th' beams of earthly kings,
   Slippery souls in smiling eyes ;
But to poor shepherds' home-spun things ;
   Whose wealth's their flock ; whose wit, to be
Well-read in their simplicity.

   Yet when young April's husband-showers
Shall bless the fruitful Maia's bed,
   We'll bring the first-born of her flowers
To kiss Thy feet, and crown Thy head.
   To Thee, dread Lamb, Whose love must
      keep
The shepherds, more than they the sheep.

[1] Butterflies, courtiers.

To 'Thee, meek Majesty, soft King
Of simple Graces and sweet Loves:
   Each of us his lamb will bring,
Each his pair of silver doves;
   Till burnt at last in fire of Thy fair eyes,
Ourselves become our own best sacrifice.

A HYMN FOR THE CIRCUMCISION
DAY OF OUR LORD

RISE, thou best and brightest morning!
   Rosy with a double red;
With thine own blush thy cheeks adorning,
   And the dear drops this day were shed.

All the purple pride, that laces
   The crimson curtains of thy bed,
Gilds thee not with so sweet graces,
   Nor sets thee in so rich a red.

Of all the fair-cheek'd flowers that fill thee,
   None so fair thy bosom strows,
As this modest maiden lily
   Our sins have shamed into a rose.

Bid thy golden god, the sun,
   Burnish'd in his best beams rise,
Put all his red-eyed rubies on;
   These rubies shall put out their eyes.

Let him make poor the purple East,
   Search what the world's close cabinets keep,
Rob the rich births of each bright nest
   That flaming in their fair beds sleep.

Let him embrave [1] his own bright tresses
  With a new morning made of gems ;
And wear, in those his wealthy dresses,
  Another day of diadems.

When he hath done all he may,
  To make himself rich in his rise,
All will be darkness to the day
  That breaks from one of these bright eyes.

And soon this sweet truth shall appear,
  Dear Babe, ere many days be done :
The Morn shall come to meet Thee here,
  And leave her own neglected sun.

Here are beauties shall bereave him [2]
  Of all his eastern paramours : [3]
His Persian lovers [3] all shall leave him,
  And swear faith to Thy sweeter powers ;
Nor while they leave him shall they lose the sun
But in Thy fairest eyes find two for one.

OUR BLESSED LORD IN HIS CIRCUMCISION TO HIS FATHER

I

TO Thee these first-fruits of My growing death,
  (For what else is My life ?) lo, I bequeath.

II

Taste this, and as Thou lik'st this lesser flood
Expect a sea ; My heart shall make it good.

[1] Decorate.   [2] The sun.
[3] The sun worshippers.

III

Thy wrath that wades here now, ere long shall
  swim,
The flood-gate shall be set wide ope for Him.

IV

Then let Him drink, and drink, and do His worst,
To drown the wantonness of His wild thirst.

V

Now's but the nonage [1] of My pains, My fears
Are yet but in their hopes, not come to years.

VI

The day of My dark woes is yet but morn,
My tears but tender, and My death new-born.

VII

Yet may these unfledged griefs give fate some
  guess,
These cradle-torments have their towardness.

VIII

These purple buds of blooming death may be
Erst the full stature of a fatal tree.

IX

And till My riper woes to age are come,
This knife may be the spear's *præludium*.[2]

[1] Not come to maturity.   [2] Prelude, type.

IN THE GLORIOUS EPIPHANY OF OUR LORD

A HYMN SUNG AS BY THE THREE KINGS

DEDICATION

TO THE QUEEN'S MAJESTY

MADAM,[1]
   'Mongst those long rows of crowns that gild
     your race,[2]
These royal sages [3] sue for decent place :
The daybreak of the Nations ; their first ray,
When the dark World dawn'd into Christian Day,
And smil'd i' th' Babe's bright face : the purpling
   bud
And rosy dawn of the right royal Blood,
Fair first-fruits of the Lamb, sure kings in this,
They took a kingdom while they gave a kiss.
But the World's homage, scarce in these well-blown,[4]
We read in you (rare Queen) ripe and full-grown.
For from this day's rich seed of diadems
Does rise a radiant crop of royal stems,
A golden harvest of crown'd heads, that meet
And crowd for kisses from the Lamb's white feet :
In this illustrious throng, your lofty flood
Swells high, fair confluence of all high-born blood :

[1] Queen Henrietta Maria, wife of Charles I.
[2] She was the daughter of Henry IV. of France.
[3] The wise men who came from the East to Christ's
cradle.
[4] Come to the full flower.

With your bright head whole groves of sceptres
    bend
Their wealthy tops, and for these feet contend.
So swore the Lamb's dread Sire, and so we see't ;
Crowns, and the heads they kiss, must court these
    feet.
Fix here, fair Majesty ! may your heart ne'er miss
To reap new crowns and kingdoms from that kiss ;
Nor may we miss the joy to meet in you
The aged honours of this day still new.
May the great time, in you, still greater be,
While all the year is your epiphany ;
While your each day's devotion duly brings
Three kingdoms to supply this day's three kings.

IN THE GLORIOUS EPIPHANY OF
OUR LORD

A HYMN SUNG AS BY THE THREE KINGS

1 *King*—**B**RIGHT Babe, Whose awful beauties
         make
    The morn incur a sweet mistake ;
2 *King*—For Whom the officious [1] Heavens devise
    To disinherit the sun's rise :
3 *King*—Delicately to displace
    The day, and plant it fairer in Thy face.
1 *King*—O Thou born King of loves,
2 *King*—Of lights,
3 *King*—Of joys,
    [1] Eager heavens devise ways, etc.

Chorus—Look up, sweet Babe, look up, and see
　　　　For love of Thee
　　　　Thus far from home
　　　　The East is come
　　To seek herself in Thy sweet eyes.

1 *King*—We, who strangely went astray,
　　　　Lost in a bright
　　　　Meridian[1] night,
2 *King*—A darkness made of too much day.
3 *King*—Beckon'd from far
　　　　By Thy fair star,
　　Lo, at last have found our way.

Chorus—To Thee, thou Day of Night, thou East
　　　　of West,
　　. 　Lo, we at last have found the way
　　　To Thee the World's great universal East,
　　　The general and indifferent[2] Day.

1 *King*—All-circling point, all-centring sphere,
　　　The World's one, round, eternal year.
2 *King*—Whose full and all-unwrinkled face
　　　Nor sinks nor swells with time or place;
3 *King*—But every where, and every while
　　　Is one consistent, solid smile.
1 *King*—Not vex'd and tost
2 *King*—'Twixt Spring and frost,
3 *King*—Nor by alternate shreds of light,
　　　Sordidly shifting hands with shades and
　　　　Night.

[1] Midnight. The highest point of the night.
[2] Impartial. Cf. the Prayer for the Church Militant in the Holy Communion Service in English Book of Common Prayer. "That they may truly and *indifferently* minister justice."

Chorus— O little All, in Thy embrace
   The World lies warm, and likes his place ;
   Nor does his full globe fail to be
   Kiss'd on both his cheeks by Thee.
   Time is too narrow for Thy year,
   Nor makes the whole World Thy half-
    sphere.

1 *King*—To Thee, to Thee
    From him we flee.

2 *King*—From him,[1] whom by a more illustrious lie,
   The blindness of the World did call the eye.

3 *King*—To Him, Who by these mortal clouds
    hast made
   Thyself our sun, though Thine Own shade.

1 *King*—Farewell, the World's false light,
    Farewell, the white
    Egypt, a long farewell to thee,
    Bright idol, black idolatry :
   The dire face of inferior darkness, kist
   And courted in the pompous mask of a
    more specious mist.

2 *King*— Farewell, farewell
    The proud and misplaced gates of
     Hell,
    Perch'd in the Morning's way,
   And double-gilded as the doors of Day :
   The deep hypocrisy of Death and Night
   More desperately dark, because more
    bright.

3 *King*— Welcome, the World's sure way,
    Heaven's wholesome ray.

Chorus— Welcome to us ; and we
    (Sweet,) to ourselves, in Thee.
     [1] The sun.

1 *King*—The deathless Heir of all Thy Father's
day;
2 *King*—   Decently [1] born,
Embosom'd in a much more rosy Morn:
The blushes of Thy all-unblemish'd Mother,
3 *King*—   No more that other
Aurora [2] shall set ope
Her ruby casements, or hereafter hope
From mortal eyes
To meet religious welcomes at her rise. [3]

Chorus—We (precious ones,) in you have won
A gentler Morn, a juster Sun.

1 *King*—His superficial beams sun-burnt our skin;
2 *King*—   But left within
3 *King*—The Night and Winter still of Death and
Sin.

Chorus—Thy softer yet more certain darts
Spare our eyes, but pierce our hearts:

1 *King*—Therefore with his proud Persian spoils
2 *King*—We court Thy more concerning smiles.
3 *King*—   Therefore with his disgrace
We gild the humble cheek of this chaste
place;

Chorus —And at Thy feet pour forth his face.

1 *King*—The doating Nations now no more
Shall any day but Thine adore.
2 *King*—Nor (much less) shall they leave these eyes
For cheap Egyptian deities.

[1] Without ostentation.   [2] The dawn.
[3] Refers to their worship of the sun.

3 *King*—In whatsoe'er more sacred shape
   Of ram, he-goat, or rev'rend ape ;
   Those beauteous ravishers oppress'd so sore
   The too-hard tempted nations :
1 *King*—   Never more
   By wanton heifer shall be worn
2 *King*—A garland, or a gilded horn :
   The altar-stall'd ox, fat Osiris [1] now
    With his fair sister cow,
3 *King*—Shall kick the clouds no more ; [2] but lean
   and tame,

Chorus— See His horn'd face, and die for shame :
   And Mithra [3] now shall be no name.

1 *King*—No longer shall the immodest lust
   Of adulterous godless dust
2 *King*—Fly in the face of Heaven ; as if it were
   The poor World's fault that He is fair.
3 *King*—Nor with perverse loves and religious rapes [4]
   Revenge Thy bounties in their beauteous
    shapes ;
   And punish best things worst, because
    they stood
   Guilty of being much for them too good.
1 *King*—Proud sons of Death, that durst compel
   Heaven itself to find them Hell :
2 *King*—And by strange wit of madness wrest
   From this World's East the other's West.

[1] An Egyptian deity, husband of Isis, goddess of the
moon.
 [2] No more shall oxen be sacrificed to the gods.
 [3] Mithras, god of the sun among the Persians. He is
represented kneeling on a bull and cutting its throat.
 [4] The actions of the pagan gods.

5

3 *King*—All-idolising worms, that thus could crowd
And urge their sun into Thy cloud;
Forcing his sometimes eclips'd face to be
A long deliquium [1] to the light of Thee.

Chorus— Alas! with how much heavier shade
The shamefaced lamp hung down his head,
For that one eclipse he made,
Than all those he suffered.

1 *King*—For this he looked so big, and ev'ry morn
With a red face confess'd his scorn;
Or, hiding his vex'd cheeks in a hired
mist,
Kept them from being so unkindly kist.

2 *King*—It was for this the Day did rise
So oft with blubber'd [2] eyes;
For this the Evening wept; and we ne'er
knew,
But called it dew.

3 *King*— This daily wrong
Silenced the morning sons, and damp'd
their song.

Chorus—Nor was't our deafness, but our sins, that
thus
Long made th' harmonious orbs all mute
to us.

1 *King*— Time has a day in store
When this so proudly poor
And self-oppressèd spark, that has so long
By the love-sick World been made
Not so much their sun as shade:
Weary of this glorious wrong,

[1] Defect, obstruction.   [2] So often misty.

From them and from himself shall flee
For shelter to the shadow of Thy Tree;[1]

Chorus— Proud to have gain'd this precious loss,
And changed his false crown for Thy
Cross.

2 *King*—That dark Day's clear doom shall define
Whose is the master Fire, which sun
should shine;
That sable judgment-seat shall by new
laws
Decide and settle the great cause
Of controverted light:[2]

Chorus— And Nature's wrongs rejoice to do Thee
right.

3 *King*—That forfeiture of Noon to Night shall pay
All the idolatrous thefts done by this
Night of Day;
And the great Penitent press his own pale
lips
With an elaborate love-eclipse:
To which the low World's laws
Shall lend no cause,

Chorus— Save those domestic which He borrows
From our sins and His Own sorrows.

1 *King*—Three sad hours' sackcloth then shall
show to us
His penance, as our fault, conspicuous:

[1] Cross.
[2] Refers to the day of the Crucifixion, on which the
sun was darkened.—Matt. xxvii. 45.

2 *King*—And He more needfully and nobly prove
  The Nations' terror now than erst their
    love ;
3 *King*—Their hated love's changed into whole-
    some fears :

Chorus— The shutting of His eye shall open theirs.

1 *King*—As by a fair-eyed fallacy of Day
    Misled before, they lost their way ;
    So shall they, by the seasonable fright
    Of an unseasonable Night,[1]
    Loosing it once again, stumble on true
      Light :
2 *King*—And as before His too-bright eye
    Was their more blind idolatry ;
    So his officious blindness now shall be
    Their black, but faithful perspective of
      Thee.
3 *King*—   His new prodigious Night,
    Their new and admirable light,
    The supernatural dawn of Thy pure Day ;
        While wondering they
    (The happy converts now of Him
    Whom they compell'd before to be their
      sin)
        Shall henceforth see
    To kiss him only as their rod,
    Whom they so long courted as God.

Chorus— And their best use of him they worshipp'd,
      be
    To learn of him at last, to worship Thee.
      [1] Matt. xxvii. 45.

1 *King*—It was their weakness woo'd his beauty;
　　　　But it shall be
　　Their wisdom now, as well as duty,
　　To enjoy his blot; and as a large black
　　　　letter
　　Use it to spell Thy beauties better;
　　And make the Night itself their torch to
　　　　Thee.

2 *King*—By the oblique ambush of this close
　　　　night
　　　　　Couch'd in that conscious shade
　　The right-eyed Areopagite [1]
　　Shall with a vigorous guess invade
　　And catch Thy quick reflex; and
　　　　sharply see
　　　　　On this dark ground
　　　　　To descant Thee.

3 *King*—O prize of the rich Spirit! with what
　　　　fierce chase
　　　　　Of his strong soul, shall he
　　　　　Leap at Thy lofty face,
　　And seize the swift flash, in rebound
　　From this obsequious cloud,
　　　　　Once call'd a sun,
　　　　　Till dearly thus undone;

Chorus— Till thus triumphantly tamed (O ye two
　　　　Twin-suns!) and taught now to negotiate
　　　　you,

1 *King*—Thus shall that rev'rend child of Light,

---

[1] Cf. Acts xvii. 16–34. The passage is too long to
quote, but Dionysius the Areopagite (the follower of one
Areopagus) was converted by Paul on Mars Hill at
Athens.

2 *King*—By being scholar first of that new Night,
Come forth great master of the mystic
Day;

3 *King*—And teach obscure mankind a more close
way,
By the frugal negative light
Of a most wise and well-abusèd Night,
To read more legible Thine original
ray;

Chorus— And make our darkness serve Thy Day,
Maintaining 'twixt Thy work and ours
A commerce of contrary powers,
A mutual trade
'Twixt sun and shade
By confederate black and white,
Borrowing Day and lending Night.

1 *King*—Thus we who when with all the noble
powers
That (at Thy cost) are called, not vainly
ours ;
We vow to make brave way
Upwards and press on for the pure
intelligential prey,

2 *King*—   At least to play
The amorous spies,
And peep and proffer at Thy sparkling
throne ;

3 *King*—Instead of bringing in the blissful prize
and fastening on Thine eyes
Forfeit our own
And nothing gain
But more ambitious loss at last, of brain.

Chorus— Now by abasèd lids shall learn to be
　　　　Eagles ; and shut our eyes that we may see.

THE CLOSE.

Chorus— Therefore to Thee and Thine auspicious
　　　　ray
　　　　　　(Dread Sweet !) lo thus
　　　　　　At last by us
　　　　The delegated eye of Day
　　　　Does first his sceptre, then himself, in
　　　　　　solemn tribute pay.
　　　　　　　　Thus he undresses
　　　　　　　　His sacred unshorn tresses ;
　　　　At Thy adorèd feet, thus he lays down

1 *King*—　　　　His gorgeous tire
　　　　　　　　Of flame and fire,

2 *King*—His glittering robe,

3 *King*—His sparkling crown ;

1 *King*—His gold,

2 *King*—His myrrh,

3 *King*—His frankincense ; [1]

Chorus— To which he now has no pretence :
　　　　For being show'd by this Day's light,
　　　　　　how far
　　　　He is from sun enough to make Thy star,
　　　　His best ambition now is but to be
　　　　Something a brighter shadow, Sweet, of
　　　　　　Thee.
　　　　Or on Heaven's azure forehead high to
　　　　　　stand
　　　　Thy golden index ; with a duteous hand
　　　　Pointing us home to our own Sun,
　　　　The world's and his Hyperion.

[1] The pure or male incense.

UPON EASTER DAY

R ISE heir of fresh Eternity,
          From thy virgin tomb.
Rise mighty Man of wonders, and Thy World with
          Thee
    Thy tomb the universal East,
      Nature's new womb,
    Thy tomb, fair Immortality's perfumèd nest.

Of all the glories make Noon gay,[1]
      This is the Morn;
This Rock buds forth the fountain of the streams
      of Day:
    In Joy's white annals lives this hour
      When Life was born;
    No cloud scowls on His radiant lids, no tempests
      lour.

Life, by this Light's nativity,
      All creatures have;
Death only by this Day's just doom is forced to
      die,
    Nor is Death forced; for may he lie
      Throned in Thy grave,
    Death will on this condition be content to die.
                    [1] That make.

SOSPETTO D'HERODE [1]

Libro Primo

ARGOMENTO

Casting the times with their strong signs,
  Death's master his own death divines ;
Struggling for help, his best hope is
  Herod's suspicion may heal his.
Therefore he sends a friend to wake
The sleeping tyrant's fond mistake,
Who fears (in vain) that He Whose birth
Means Heaven, should meddle with his Earth.

1

MUSE, now the servant of soft loves no more,
    Hate is thy theme, and Herod, whose
        unblest
Hand (O, what dares not jealous greatness ?) tore
  A thousand sweet babes from their mothers'
      breast,
The blooms of martyrdom.   O, be a door
  Of language to my infant lips, ye best
    Of Confessors ; whose throats, answering his
      swords,
    Gave forth your blood for breath, spoke souls
      for words.

[1] The jealousy of Herod.   A poem in Italian by
Marino, called "Strage degli Innocenti," Book I., of
which this is a very free translation.

II

Great Anthony,[1] Spain's well-beseeming pride,
  Thou mighty branch of emperors and kings;
The beauties of whose dawn what eye may bide?
  Which with the sun himself weighs equal wings;
Map of heroic worth, whom far and wide
  To the believing world Fame boldly sings:
    Deign thou to wear this humble wreath that
      bows,
    To be the sacred honour of thy brows.

III

Nor needs my Muse a blush, or these bright flowers
  Other than what their own blest beauties bring;
They were the smiling sons of those sweet bowers,
  That drink the dew of life, whose deathless
    spring,
Nor Syrian flame, nor Borean[2] frost deflowers:
  From whence heaven-labouring bees with busy
    wing,
    Suck hidden sweets, which, well digested,
      prove
    Immortal honey for the hive of love.

[1] Anthony.   I think this refers to St. Anthony of
Padua, who was born at Lisbon, however, in Portugal.
This is very interesting, however, for Spain seized Portugal
in 1580, and the Portuguese did not get back their kingdom
till the treaty of Lisbon, 1668.   As Crashaw died in 1648,
he of course calls all that peninsula Spain.   At the same
time we must remember that Crashaw is here supposed
to be translating.
  [2] Northern.

IV

Thou, whose strong hand with so transcendent
    worth,
  Holds high the reign of fair Parthenope,[1]
That neither Rome nor Athens can bring forth
  A name in noble deeds rival to thee!
Thy fame's full noise makes proud the patient
    Earth,
    Far more than matter for my Muse and me.
      The Tyrrhene [2] Seas and shores sound all the
        same,
      And in their murmurs kept thy mighty name.

V

Below the bottom of the great Abyss,
  There where one centre reconciles all things,
The World's profound heart pants; there placèd is
  Mischief's old master: close about him clings
A curled knot of embracing snakes, that kiss
  His correspondent cheeks: these loathsome strings
    Hold the perverse Prince in eternal ties
    Fast bound, since first he forfeited the skies.

VI

The Judge of torments, and the King of tears,
  He fills a burnish'd throne of quenchless fire:
And for his old fair robes of light he wears
  A gloomy mantle of dark flames; the tire

[1] Naples.
[2] That part of the Mediterranean between Italy, Corsica,
Sardinia, and Sicily.

That crowns his hated head on high appears ;
  Where seven tall horns (his empire's pride)
    aspire ;
    And to make up Hell's Majesty, each horn
    Seven crested Hydras horribly adorn.

VII

His eyes, the sullen dens of Death and Night,
  Startle the dull air with a dismal red :
Such his fell glances as the fatal light
  Of staring comets, that look kingdoms dead.
From his black nostrils and blue lips, in spite
  Of Hell's own stink, a worser stench is spread.
    His breath Hell's lightning is : and each deep
      groan
    Disdains to think that Heaven thunders alone.

VIII

His flaming eyes' dire exhalation
  Unto a dreadful pile gives fiery breath ;
Whose unconsumed consumption preys upon
  The never-dying life of a long death.
In this sad house of slow destruction
  (His shop of flames) he fries himself, beneath
    A mass of woes ; his teeth for torment gnash,
    While his steel sides sound with his tail's
      strong lash.

IX

Three rigorous virgins waiting still behind,
  Assist the throne of th' iron-sceptred King :

With whips of thorns and knotty vipers twined
   They rouse him, when his rank thoughts need a
      sting.
Their locks are beds of uncombed snakes, that wind
   About their shady brows in wanton rings.
      Thus reigns the wrathful King, and while he
        reigns,
      His sceptre and himself both he disdains.

x

Disdainful wretch, how hath one bold sin cost
   Thee all the beauties of thy once bright eyes.
How hath one black eclipse cancelled and crost
   The glories that did gild thee in thy rise.
Proud Morning [1] of a perverse day, how lost
   Art thou unto thyself, thou too self-wise
      Narcissus, foolish Phaethon, who for all
        Thy high-aim'd hopes gain'dst but a flaming
        fall.

xi

From Death's sad shades to the life-breathing
      air,
   This mortal enemy to mankind's good,
Lifts his malignant eyes, wasted with care,
   To become beautiful in human blood.
Where Jordan melts his crystal, to make fair
   The fields of Palestine, with so pure a flood,
      There does he fix his eyes, and there detect
      New matter, to make good his great suspect.

[1] Satan is called the son of the morning, Isaiah xiv. 12 :
" How art thou fallen . . . Lucifer, son of the morning ! "

XII

He calls to mind th' old quarrel, and what spark
    Set the contending sons of Heaven on fire;
Oft in his deep thought he revolves the dark
    Sybil's divining leaves: he does inquire
Into th' old prophecies, trembling to mark
      How many present prodigies conspire
        To crown their past predictions; both he lays
        Together; in his ponderous mind both weighs.

XIII

Heaven's golden-wingèd herald,[1] late he saw
    To a poor Galilean virgin sent:
How low the bright youth bowed, and with what
        awe
Immortal flowers to her fair hand present.
He saw th' old Hebrew's [2] womb neglect the law
    Of age and barrenness, and her babe prevent [3]
      His birth by his devotion, who began
      Betimes to be a saint, before a man. [4]

XIV

He saw rich nectar-thaws release the rigour
    Of th' icy North; from frost-bound Atlas' [5]
    hands

[1] The angel Gabriel.
[2] Elisabeth, mother of St. John the Baptist.
[3] Anticipate. Cf. the collect in Book of Common Prayer: "Prevent us, O Lord, in all our doings."
[4] Cf. Luke i. 41.
[5] Atlas was, according to the legend, changed into the mountain of that name by Perseus by means of Medusa's head.

His adamantine fetters fall : green vigour
  Gladding the Scythian rocks and Libyan sands.
He saw a vernal smile sweetly disfigure
  Winter's sad face, and through the flowery lands
    Of fair Engaddi, honey-sweating fountains
    With manna, milk, and balm, new-broach the
      mountains.

xv

He saw how, in that blest Day-bearing night,
  The Heaven-rebukèd shades made haste away ;
How bright a dawn of angels with new light
  Amazed the midnight world, and made a Day
Of which the Morning knew not ; mad with spite
  He marked how the poor shepherds ran to pay
    Their simple tribute to the Babe, Whose
      birth
    Was the great business both of Heaven and
      Earth.

xvi

He saw a threefold Sun, with rich increase,
  Make proud the ruby portals of the East :
He saw the Temple sacred to sweet Peace,
  Adore her Prince's birth, flat on her breast :
He saw the falling idols all confess
  A coming Deity : He saw the nest
    Of poisonous and unnatural loves, Earth-
      nursed,
    Touched with the World's true antidote, to
      burst.

XVII

He saw Heaven blossom with a new-born light,
  On which, as on a glorious stranger, gazed
The golden eyes of Night : whose beam made
    bright
  The way to Bethlehem, and as boldly blazed,
(Nor asked leave of the sun) by day as night ;
    By whom (as Heaven's illustrious handmaid)
    raised,
      Three kings (or what is more) three wise
      men went
      Westward to find the World's true Orient.

XVIII

Struck with these great concurrences of things,
  Symptoms so deadly unto Death and him,
Fain would he have forgot what fatal strings
  Eternally bind each rebellious limb.
He shook himself, and spread his spacious wings ;
    Which, like two bosomed sails,[1] embrace the
    dim
      Air with a dismal shade ; but all in vain,
      Of sturdy adamant [2] is his strong chain.

XIX

While thus Heaven's highest counsels by the low
  Footsteps of their effects, he traced too well,
He tossed his troubled eyes, embers that glow
  Now with new rage, and wax too hot for Hell.

[1] Cf. *Paradise Lost*, II. 927–930.
[2] Cf. *Paradise Lost*, I. 48.

With his foul claws he fenced his furrowed brow,
   And gave a ghastly shriek,[1] whose horrid yell
     Ran trembling through the hollow vaults of
      ' Night,
   The while his twisted tail he gnawed for spite.

XX

Yet on the other side fain would he start
   Above his fears, and think it cannot be:
He studies Scripture, strives to sound the heart,
   And feel the pulse of every prophecy.
He knows (but knows not how, or by what art)
   The Heaven-expecting ages hope to see
     A mighty Babe, Whose pure, unspotted birth,
     From a chaste virgin womb should bless the
      Earth.

XXI

But these vast mysteries his senses smother,
   And reason (for what's faith to him?) devour,
How She that is a maid should prove a mother,
   Yet keep inviolate her virgin flower;
How God's Eternal Son should be man's brother,
   Poseth his proudest intellectual power;
     How a pure Spirit should incarnate be,
     And Life itself wear Death's frail livery.

XXII

That the great angel-blinding Light should shrink
   His blaze, to shine in a poor shepherd's eye;
That the unmeasured God so low should sink,
   As prisoner in a few poor rags to lie;

[1] Cf. *Paradise Lost*, I. 542-643.

6

That from His Mother's breast He milk should
    drink,
  Who feeds with nectar Heaven's fair family ;
    That a vile manger His low bed should prove,
    Who in a throne of stars thunders above ;

XXIII

That He Whom the Sun serves should faintly peep
  Through clouds of infant flesh : that He, the old
Eternal Word, should be a child, and weep :
    That He Who made the fire, should fear the
      cold :
That Heaven's High Majesty His court should
    keep
    In a clay-cottage, by each blast controll'd :
      That Glory's Self should serve our griefs and
        fears :
      And free Eternity submit to years :

XXIV

And further, that the Law's eternal Giver
  Should bleed in His Own law's obedience :
And to the circumcising knife deliver
  Himself, the forfeit of His slave's offence.
That the unblemish'd Lamb, blessèd for ever,
  Should take the mark of sin, and pain of sense :
    These are the knotty riddles, whose dark
      doubt
    Entangles his lost thoughts, past getting out.

XXV

While new thoughts boiled in his enragèd breast,
  His gloomy bosom's darkest character

Was in his shady forehead seen exprest.
The forehead's shade in Grief's expression there,
Is what in sign of joy among the blest
The face's lightning, or a smile is here.
Those stings of care that his strong heart
opprest,
A desperate, " Oh me ! " drew from his deep
breast.

XXVI

" Oh me ! " (thus bellow'd he) " Oh me ! what
great
Portents before mine eyes their powers advance ?
And serves my purer sight only to beat
Down my proud thought, and leave it in a
trance ?
Frown I ; and can great Nature keep her seat,
And the gay stars lead on their golden dance ?
Can His attempts above still prosperous be,
Auspicious still, in spite of Hell and me ?

XXVII

" He has my Heaven [1] (what would He more ?)
whose bright
And radiant sceptre this bold hand should bear,
And for the never-fading fields of light,
My fair inheritance, He confines me here,
To this dark house of shades, horror, and night,
To draw a long-lived death, where all my cheer
Is the solemnity my sorrow wears,
That mankind's torment waits upon my tears.

[1] Isaiah xiv. 12.

XXVIII

" Dark, dusky Man, He needs would single forth,
   To make the partner of His Own pure ray :
And should we powers of Heaven, spirits of worth,
   Bow our bright heads before a king of clay ?
It shall not be, said I, and clomb the North,[1]
   Where never wing of angel yet made way.
      What though I miss'd my blow ? yet I struck
        high,
      And to dare something is some victory.[2]

XXIX

" Is He not satisfied ? means He to wrest
   Hell from me too, and sack my territories ?
Vile human nature, means He not t' invest
   (O my despite !) with His divinest glories ?
And rising with rich spoils upon His breast,
   With His fair triumphs fill all future stories ?
      Must the bright arms of Heaven rebuke these
        eyes,
      Mock me, and dazzle my dark mysteries ?

XXX

" Art thou not Lucifer ? he to whom the droves
   Of stars that gild the Morn, in charge were
      given ?
The nimblest of the lightning-wingèd loves,
   The fairest, and the first-born smile of Heaven ?
Look in what pomp the mistress planet moves
   Reverently circled by the lesser seven ;

[1] Isaiah xiv. 13 : " In the sides of the north."
[2] Cf. *Paradise Lost*, i. 105–108.

Such, and so rich, the flames that from thine
  eyes
Oppressed the common people of the skies.

XXXI

"Ah, wretch, what boots thee to cast back thy
    eyes,
  Where dawning hope no beam of comfort
    shows?
While the reflection of thy forepast joys,
  Renders thee double to thy present woes;
Rather make up to thy new miseries,
  And meet the mischief that upon thee grows;
    If Hell must mourn, Heaven sure shall sym-
      pathise;
    What force cannot effect, fraud shall devise.

XXXII

"And yet whose force fear I? have I so lost
  Myself? my strength too with my innocence?
Come, try who dares, Heaven, Earth, whate'er
    doth boast
  A borrowed being, make thy bold defence:
Come thy Creator too; what though it cost
  Me yet a second fall? we'd try our strengths;
    Heaven saw us struggle once; as brave a fight
    Earth now should see, and tremble at the
      sight."

XXXIII

Thus spoke th' impatient Prince, and made a pause;
  His foul hags raised their heads, and clapped
    their hands;

And all the powers of Hell in full applause
  Flourish'd their snakes and tossed their flaming
    brands.
"We" (said the horrid sisters) "wait thy laws,
  Th' obsequious handmaids of thy high com-
    mands ;
    Be it thy part, Hell's mighty lord, to lay
    On us thy dread commands, ours to obey.

XXXIV

"What thy Alecto,[1] what these hands can do,
  Thou madest bold proof upon the brow of
    Heaven,
Nor should'st thou bate [2] in pride, because that now,
  To these thy sooty kingdoms thou art driven :
Let Heaven's Lord chide above, louder than thou
  In language of His thunder, thou art even
    With Him below : here thou art lord alone,
    Boundless and absolute : Hell is thine own.

XXXV

"If usual wit and strength will do no good,
  Virtues of stones, nor herbs : use stronger charms,
Anger, and love, best hooks of human blood :
  If all fail, we'll put on our proudest arms,
And pouring on Heaven's face the Sea's huge flood,
  Quench His curled fires; we'll wake with our
    alarms
    Ruin, where'er she sleeps at Nature's feet ;
    And crush the World till His wide corners
    meet." [3]

[1] One of the Furies.   [2] Grow less.
[3] Rev. vii. 1.

XXXVI

Replied the proud king, "O my crown's defence,
   Stay of my strong hopes, you, of whose brave
      worth,
The frighted stars took faint experience,
   When 'gainst the Thunder's mouth we marchèd
      forth :
Still you are prodigal of your Love's expense
   In our great projects, both 'gainst Heaven and
      Earth :
    I thank you all, but one must single out :
    Cruelty, she alone shall cure my doubt."

XXXVII

Fourth of the cursèd knot of hags is she,
   Or rather all the other three in one ;
Hell's shop of slaughter she does oversee,
   And still assist the execution :
But chiefly there does she delight to be,
   Where Hell's capacious cauldron is set on :
    And while the black souls boil in their own
      gore,
    To hold them down, and look that none
    seethe o'er.

XXXVIII

Thrice howled the caves of Night, and thrice the
    sound,
   Thundering upon the banks of those black
    lakes,
Rung through the hollow vaults of Hell profound :
   At last her listening ears the noise o'ertakes,

She lifts her sooty lamps, and looking round,
   A general hiss from the whole tire of snakes
     Rebounding, through Hell's inmost caverns
      came,
   In answer to her formidable name.

XXXIX

'Mongst all the palaces in Hell's command,
   No one so merciless as this of hers.
The adamantine doors for ever stand
   Impenetrable, both to prayers and tears ;
The walls' inexorable steel, no hand
   Of Time, or teeth of hungry Ruin fears.
     Their ugly ornaments are the bloody stains
     Of ragged limbs, torn skulls, and dashed-out
      brains.

XL

There has the purple Vengeance a proud seat,
   Whose ever-brandish'd sword is sheathed in
     blood :
About her Hate, Wrath, War, and Slaughter
     sweat,
   Bathing their hot limbs in life's precious flood.
There rude impetuous Rage does storm and fret :
   And there, as master of this murdering brood,
     Swinging a huge scythe, stands impartial
      Death,
     With endless business almost out of breath.

XLI

For hangings and for curtains, all along
   The walls (abominable ornaments)

Are tools of wrath, anvils of torments hung ;
  Fell executioners of foul intents,
Nails, hammers, hatchets sharp, and halters strong,
  Swords, spears, with all the fatal instruments
      Of Sin and Death, twice dipped in the dire
        stains
      Of brothers' mutual blood, and fathers' brains.

XLII

The tables furnished with a cursèd feast,
  Which Harpies [1] with lean Famine feed upon,
Unfilled for ever.   Here among the rest,
  Inhuman Erisichthon,[2] too, makes one ;
Tantalus,[3] Atreus,[4] Procne,[5] here are guests :
  Wolfish Lycaon [6] here a place hath won.
      The cup they drink in is Medusa's [7] skull,
      Which, mixed with gall and blood, they
        quaff brimful.

The Harpies or Robbers and Spoilers. They are represented as winged maidens, or as birds with the heads of maidens. They tormented Phineus whenever food was placed before him by darting down and carrying it off.

[2] Son of Trispar, who was condemned to eat his own flesh.

[3] Punished by Zeus for divulging his secrets, he was placed beside a lake he could not approach, tormented by a raging thirst.

[4] Atreus. The head of the great family celebrated in Greek tragedy. He caused Thyestes to eat the flesh of his sons.

[5] Proco, according to Ovid (*Met.* vi. 565), killed her own son Itys and gave his flesh to Tereus to eat.

[6] King of Arcadia, who when visited by Zeus gave him a dish of human flesh.

[7] The third of the Gorgons, the only one of the three sisters that was mortal. To look on her was to be turned to stone, so frightful was she. Perseus slew her.

XLIII

The foul queen's most abhorrèd maids of honour,
  Medæa, Jezebel,[1] many a meagre witch,
With Circe,[2] Scylla,[3] stand to wait upon her ;
  But her best housewives are the Parcæ,[4] which
Still work for her, and have their wages from her ;
  They prick a bleeding heart at every stitch.
    Her cruel clothes of costly threads they weave,
    Which short-cut lives of murdered infants
    leave.

XLIV

The house is hearsed about with a black wood,
  Which nods with many a heavy-headed tree :
Each flower's a pregnant poison, tried and good :
  Each herb a plague : the wind's sighs timèd be
By a black fount, which weeps into a flood.
  Through the thick shades obscurely might you
    see
    Minotaurs,[5] Cyclopes,[6] with a dark drove
    Of Dragons, Hydras,[7] Sphinxes,[8] fill the grove.

[1] 1 Kings xvi. 31.
[2] An enchantress encountered by Ulysses.
[3] A monster dwelling in a cave on the Italian coast opposite Sicily.
[4] The three Fates.
[5] A monster half man half bull slain by Theseus with the help of Ariadne.
[6] The mighty assistants of Hephaestos (Vulcan).
[7] Monsters with nine heads. When Hercules cut off one two came in its place.
[8] A monster like a winged lion, but with the breast and head of a woman.

XLV

Here Diomed's [1] horses, Phereus' [2] dogs appear,
　With the fierce lions of Therodamas ; [3]
Busiris [4] has his bloody altar here,
　Here Sylla [5] his severest prison has ;
The Lestrigonians [6] here their table rear ;
　　Here strong Procrustes [7] plants his bed of brass ;
　　　Here cruel Scyron [8] boasts his bloody rocks,
　　　And hateful Schinis [9] his so fearèd oaks.

XLVI

Whatever schemes of blood, fantastic frames
　Of death Mezentius, [10] or Geryon [11] drew ;

[1] A supposed tamer of horses.

[2] Alexander of Pheræ, a Thessalian tyrant of the fourth century, B.C.

[3] Is said to have been King of Numidia or Scythia, who fed lions with the flesh of men. Cf. Ovid, *Epist. ex Ponto*, I. 2. 119.

[4] A King of Egypt who sacrificed strangers to Zeus.

[5] Possibly a robber slain by Theseus. On the other hand, it may refer to Sylla the Dictator ; but the apparent derivation from συλάω would suggest that Sylla was the name of a robber.

[6] A tribe of giants who ate one of the companions of Ulysses.

[7] A robber who tied all travellers he caught to a bed, and stretched them to its length if they were too short, or cut off their legs if too long.

[8] A robber who infested the frontier between Attica and Mageris. From the Scironian rock he kicked his victims into the sea.

[9] Usually written Sinis, one of the robbers who used to tear his victims to pieces by binding them to the tops of trees bent down and then suddenly let go ; slain by Theseus.

[10] King of Agylla, expelled by his subjects for cruelty.

[11] A monster with three heads carried off by Hercules.

Phalaris,[1] Ochus,[2] Ezelinus,[3] names
  Mighty in mischief, with dread Nero too ;
Here are they all, here all the swords or flames
  Assyrian tyrants or Egyptian knew.
    Such was the house, so furnished was the hall,
    Whence the fourth Fury answered Pluto's call.

XLVII

Scarce to this monster could the shady [4] King
  The horrid sum of his intentions tell ;
But she (swift as the momentary wing
  Of lightning, or the words he spoke) left Hell.
She rose, and with her to our World did bring
  Pale proof of her fell presence ; th' air too well
    With a changed countenance witnessed the sight,
    And poor fowls intercepted in their flight.

XLVIII

Heaven saw her rise, and saw Hell in her sight.
  The fields' fair eyes [5] saw her, and saw no more,
But shut their flowery lids for ever ; Night
  And Winter strow her way ; yea, such a sore
Is she to Nature, that a general fright,
  An universal palsy spreading o'er
    The face of things, from her dire eyes had run,
    Had not her thick snakes hid them from the sun.

[1] A ruler of Agrigentum famous for cruelty.
[2] Artaxerxes III., King of Persia.
[3] Ezzelino or Eccelino da Romano, Lord of Padua,
was a most ferocious tyrant in the 13th century. Cf.
Browning's *Sordello*, bk. vi.—

       "Grey, wizened, dwarfish devil Ecelin."

[4] King of the shades or disembodied spirits. Hades
or Pluto.
[5] The flowers.

XLIX

Now had the Night's companion from her den,
  Where all the busy day she close doth lie,
With her soft wing wiped from the brows of men
  Day's sweat, and by a gentle tyranny,
And sweet oppression, kindly cheating them
  Of all their cares, tamed the rebellious eye
    Of Sorrow, with a soft and downy hand,
    Sealing all breasts in a Lethean band.

L

When the Erinnys [1] her black pinions spread,
  And came to Bethlehem, where the cruel king
Had now retired himself, and borrowèd
  His breast awhile from Care's unquiet sting;
Such as at Thebes' dire feast she showed her head,
  Her sulphur-breathèd torches brandishing;
    Such to the frighted palace now she comes,
    And with soft feet searches the silent rooms.

LI

By Herod —— now was borne
  The sceptre, which of old great David swayed;
Whose right by David's lineage so long worn,
  Himself a stranger to, his own had made;
And from the head of Judah's house quite torn
  The crown, for which upon their necks he laid
    A sad yoke, under which they sighed in vain,
    And looking on their lost state sighed again.

[1] The goddess of vengeance.

LII

Up through the spacious palace passèd she
  To where the king's proudly-reposèd head
(If any can be soft to Tyranny
  And self-tormenting sin) had a soft bed.
She thinks not fit such he her face should see,
  As it is seen in Hell, and seen with dread;
    To change her face's style she doth devise,
    And in a pale ghost's shape to spare his eyes.

LIII

Herself a while she lays aside, and makes
  Ready to personate a mortal part.
Joseph, the king's dead brother's shape, she takes;
  What he by nature was, is she by art,
She comes to th' king, and with her cold hand slakes
  His spirits the sparks of life, and chills his heart,
    Life's forge; feigned is her voice, and false
      too be
    Her words: "Sleep'st thou, fond man?
      sleep'st thou?" said she.

LIV

"So sleeps a pilot whose poor bark is prest
  With many a merciless o'ermastering wave;
For whom (as dead) the wrathful winds contest,
  Which of them deep'st shall dig her watery
    grave.
Why dost thou let thy brave soul lie supprest
  In death-like slumbers, while thy dangers crave
    A waking eye and hand? look up and see
    The Fates ripe, in their great conspiracy.

LV

" Know'st thou not how of th' Hebrew's royal
  stem
(That old dry stock) a despaired branch is sprung,
A most strange Babe ; Who here concealed by them
  In a neglected stable lies, among
Beasts and base straw : already is the stream
  Quite turn'd : th' ingrateful rebels this their
    young
    Master (with voice free as the trump of
      Fame)
    Their new King, and thy Successor proclaim.

LVI

" What busy motions, what wild engines stand
  On tiptoe in their giddy brains ; they've fire
Already in their bosoms ; and their hand
  Already reaches at a sword : they hire
Poisons to speed thee ; yet through all the Land
  What one comes to reveal what they conspire ?
    Go now, make much of these ; wage still
      their wars,
    And bring home on thy breast more thankless
      scars.

LVII

" Why did I spend my life, and spill my blood,
  That thy firm hand for ever might sustain
A well-poised sceptre ? Does it now seem good
  Thy brother's blood be spilt, life spent in vain ?
'Gainst thy own sons and brothers thou hast stood
  In arms, when lesser cause was to complain :

And now cross Fates a watch about thee
   keep.
    Canst thou be careless now ? now canst thou
   sleep ?

LVIII

"Where art thou, man ? what cowardly mistake
   Of thy great self hath stolen king Herod from
   thee ?
O, call thyself home to thyself ; wake, wake,
   And fence the hanging sword Heaven throws
    upon thee :
Redeem a worthy wrath, rouse thee, and shake
   Thyself into a shape that may become thee.
    Be Herod, and thou shalt not miss from me
    Immortal stings to thy great thoughts, and
    thee."

LIX

So said, her richest snake, which to her wrist
   For a beseeming bracelet she had tied
(A special worm it was as ever kissed
   The foamy lips of Cerberus [1]), she applied
To the king's heart ; the snake no sooner hissed
   But Virtue heard it, and away she hied.
    Dire flames diffuse themselves through every
    vein ;
    This done, home to her Hell she hied amain.

LX

He wakes, and with him (ne'er to sleep) new
   fears :
   His sweat-bedewèd bed hath now betrayed him

[1] The three-headed dog that guarded the gate of Hades.
Around his necks snakes coiled.

To a vast field of thorns; ten thousand spears
  All pointed in his heart seemed to invade him:
So mighty were th' amazing characters
  With which his feeling dream had thus dis-
    mayed him,
    He his own fancy-framèd foes defies:
    In rage, "My arms, give me my arms," he
    cries.

LXI

As when a pile of food-preparing fire
  The breath of artificial lungs embraves,
The cauldron-prisoned waters straight conspire,
  And beat the hot brass with rebellious waves;
He murmurs, and rebukes their bold desire;
    Th' impatient liquor frets, and foams, and raves,
    Till his o'erflowing pride suppress the flame,
    Whence all his high spirits and hot courage
    came.

LXII

So boils the firèd Herod's blood-swollen breast,
  Not to be slaked but by a sea of blood.
His faithless crown he feels loose on his crest,
  Which on false tyrant's head ne'er firmly stood.
The worm of jealous envy and unrest,
    To which his gnawed heart is the growing
    food,
    Makes him impatient of the lingering light,
    Hate the sweet peace of all-composing Night.

LXIII

A thousand prophecies, that talk strange things,
  Had sown of old these doubts in his deep breast;

7

And now of late came tributary kings,
  Bringing him nothing but new fears from th'
        East,
More deep suspicions, and more deadly stings,
  With which his feverous cares their cold in-
      creased ;
    And now his dream (Hell's firebrand), still
      more bright,
    Showed him his fears, and killed him with the
    sight.

LXIV

No sooner therefore shall the Morning see
  (Night hangs yet heavy on the lids of Day),
But all the counsellors must summoned be
  To meet their troubled lord : without delay
Heralds and messengers immediately
  Are sent about, who posting every way
    To th' heads and officers of every band,
    Declare who sends, and what is his command.

LXV

Why art thou troubled, Herod? what vain fear
  Thy blood-revolving breast to rage doth move?
Heaven's King, Who doffs Himself weak flesh to
    wear,
  Comes not to rule in wrath, but serve in love :
Nor would He this thy feared crown from thee
    tear,
  But give thee a better with Himself above.
    Poor jealousy ! why should He wish to prey
    Upon thy crown, Who gives His own away?

Make to thy reason, man, and mock thy doubts;
  Look how below thy fears their causes are;
Thou art a soldier, Herod; send thy scouts,
  See how He's furnished for so feared a war.
What armour does He wear? a few thin clouts.
  His trumpets? tender cries. His men, to dare
    So much? rude shepherds. What His steeds?
      alas,
    Poor beasts! a slow ox and a simple ass.

IL FINE DEL PRIMO LIBRO.

THE HYMN OF ST. THOMAS

IN ADORATION OF THE BLESSED SACRAMENT

Ecce Panis Angelorum: Adoro Te

WITH all the powers my poor heart hath
  Of humble love and loyal faith,
Thus low (my hidden life) I bow to Thee,
Whom too much love hath bow'd more low for me.
Down, down, proud Sense, discourses die,
Keep close, my soul's inquiring eye;
Nor Touch nor Taste must look for more,
But each sit still in his own door.

  Your ports[1] are all superfluous here,
Save that which lets in Faith, the ear.
Faith is my skill; Faith can believe
As fast as Love new laws can give.
Faith is my force: Faith strength affords
To keep pace with those pow'rful words.

      [1] Gates—doors.

And words more sure, more sweet than they,
Love could not think, Truth could not say.

O let Thy wretch find that relief
Thou didst afford the faithful thief.
Plead for me, Love! allege and show
That Faith has farther here to go,
And less to lean on: because then
Though hid as God, wounds writ Thee man;
Thomas might touch, none but might see
At least the suffering side of Thee;
And that too was Thyself which Thee did cover,
But here ev'n that's hid too which hides the other.

Sweet, consider then, that I,
Though allowed nor hand nor eye
To reach at Thy loved face; nor can
Taste Thee God, or touch Thee Man,
Both yet believe, and witness Thee
My Lord too, and my God, as loud as he.

Help, Lord, my faith, my hope increase,
And fill my portion in Thy peace:
Give love for life; nor let my days
Grow, but in new powers to Thy Name and Praise.

O dear memorial of that Death
Which lives still, and allows us breath,
Rich, Royal Food, Bountiful Bread,
Whose use denies us to the dead;
Whose vital gust alone can give
The same leave both to eat and live.
Live ever, Bread of loves, and be
My life, my soul, my surer self to me.

O soft, self-wounding Pelican,[1]
Whose breast weeps balm for wounded man:
Ah, this way bend Thy benign flood
To a bleeding heart that gasps for blood.
That blood, whose least drops sovereign be
To wash my worlds of sins from me.

Come Love! come Lord! and that long day
For which I languish, come away.
When this dry soul those eyes shall see,
And drink the unseal'd source of Thee:
When Glory's sun, Faith's shades shall chase,
And for Thy veil give me Thy face.   Amen.

LAUDA SION SALVATOREM

THE HYMN FOR THE BLESSED SACRAMENT

I

RISE, royal Sion! rise and sing
    Thy soul's kind Shepherd, thy heart's King.
Stretch all thy powers; call if you can
Harps of heaven to hands of man.
This sovereign subject sits above
The best ambition of thy love.

II

Lo, the Bread of Life, this day's
Triumphant text, provokes thy praise;
The Living and Life-giving Bread,
To the great twelve distributed;
When Life, Himself, at point to die
Of love, was His Own legacy.

[1] An emblem of Christ: so used by Dante.

III

Come, Love! and let us work a song
Loud and pleasant, sweet and long;
Let lips and hearts lift high the noise
Of so just and solemn joys,
Which on His white brows this bright day
Shall hence for ever bear away.

IV

Lo, the new law of a new Lord,
With a new Lamb blesses the board:
The agèd Pascha pleads not years,
But spies Love's dawn, and disappears.
Types yield to truths;[1] shades shrink away;
And their Night dies into our Day.

V

But lest that die too, we are bid
Ever to do what He once did:
And by a mindful, mystic breath,
That we may live, revive His Death;
With a well-bless'd Bread and Wine,
Transumed,[2] and taught to turn Divine.

VI

The Heaven-instructed house of Faith
Here a holy dictate hath,
That they but lend their form and face;
Themselves with reverence leave their place,

[1] Cf. "Et antiquum documentum novo cedat ritui" of the "Tantum Ergo."
[2] Changed, converted.

Nature, and name, to be made good,
By a nobler Bread, more needful Blood.

VII

Where Nature's laws no leave will give,
Bold Faith takes heart, and dares believe
In different Species : name not things,
Himself to me my Saviour brings ;
As meat in that, as drink in this,
But still in both one Christ He is.

VIII

The receiving mouth here makes
Nor wound nor breach in What he takes.
Let one, or one thousand be
Here dividers, single he
Bears home no less, all they no more,
Nor leave they both less than before.

IX

Though in Itself this sov'reign Feast
Be all the same to every guest,
Yet on the same (life-meaning) Bread
The child of death eats himself dead :
Nor is't Love's fault, but Sin's dire skill
That thus from Life can death distil.

X

When the blest Signs thou broke shalt see,
Hold but thy faith entire as He,
Who, howsoe'er clad, cannot come
Less than whole Christ in every crumb.

In broken forms a stable Faith
Untouch'd her precious total hath.

XI

Lo, the Life-food of angels then
Bow'd to the lowly mouths of men ;
The children's Bread, the Bridegroom's Wine,
Not to be cast to dogs or swine.

XII

Lo, the full, final Sacrifice
On which all figures fix'd their eyes :
The ransom'd Isaac, and his ram ;
The manna, and the paschal lamb.

XIII

Jesu Master, just and true,
Our Food, and faithful Shepherd too ;
O by Thyself vouchsafe to keep,
As with Thyself Thou feed'st Thy sheep.

XIV

O let that love which thus makes Thee
Mix with our low mortality,
Lift our lean souls, and set us up
Convictors of Thine Own full cup,
Coheirs of Saints.   That so all may
Drink the same wine ; and the same way :
Not change the pasture, but the place,
To feed of Thee in Thine Own Face.   Amen.

PRAYER

AN ODE WHICH WAS PREFIXED TO A LITTLE PRAYER-
BOOK GIVEN TO A YOUNG GENTLEWOMAN

LO here a little volume, but great book!
  (Fear it not, sweet,
   It is no hypocrite),
Much larger in itself than in its look.
  A nest of new-born sweets;
  Whose native fires disdaining
  To lie thus folded, and complaining
  Of these ignoble sheets,
  Affect more comely bands
  (Fair one) from thy kind hands;
  And confidently look
  To find the rest
Of a rich binding in your breast.
It is, in one choice handful, Heaven and all
Heaven's royal host; encamp'd thus small
To prove that true, Schools use to tell,
Ten thousand angels in one point can dwell.
It is Love's great artillery
Which here contracts itself, and comes to lie
Close-couch'd in your white bosom; and from
   thence,
As from a snowy fortress of defence,
Against the ghostly foes to take your part,
And fortify the hold of your chaste heart.
It is an armoury of light;
Let constant use but keep it bright,
  You'll find it yields,

To holy hands and humble hearts,
  More swords and shields
Than sin hath snares, or Hell hath darts.
  Only be sure
  The hands be pure
That hold these weapons; and the eyes
  Those of turtles,[1] chaste and true;
Wakeful and wise:
  Here is a friend shall fight for you,
Hold but this book before your heart,
Let Prayer alone to play his part;
But O the heart,
That studies this high art,
Must be a sure house-keeper:
And yet no sleeper.
Dear soul, be strong,
Mercy will come ere long,
And bring his bosom fraught with blessings,
Flowers of never-fading graces,
To make immortal dressings
For worthy souls, whose wise embraces
Store up themselves for Him, Who is alone
The Spouse of virgins, and the Virgin's Son.
But if the noble Bridegroom, when He come,
  Shall find the loitering heart from home;
  Leaving her chaste abode
  To gad abroad
Among the gay mates of the god of flies;[2]
  To take her pleasure, and to play
  And keep the devil's holiday;
To dance in th' sunshine of some smiling
  But beguiling

[1] Turtle doves.
[2] Beelzebub. Cf. *Paradise Lost*, II. 299.

Sphere of sweet and sugar'd lies;
    Some slippery pair,
    Of false, perhaps as fair,
Flattering but forswearing, eyes;
Doubtless some other heart
    Will get the start
Meanwhile, and stepping in before,
Will take possession of the sacred store
Of hidden sweets and holy joys;
Words which are not heard with ears
(Those tumultuous shops of noise)
Effectual whispers, whose still voice
The soul itself more feels than hears;
Amorous languishments, luminous trances;
Sights which are not seen with eyes;
Spiritual and soul-piercing glances,
Whose pure and subtle lightning flies
Home to the heart, and sets the house on fire
And melts it down in sweet desire:
    Yet does not stay
To ask the windows' leave to pass that way;
Delicious deaths, soft exhalations
Of soul; dear and divine annihilations;
    A thousand unknown rites
    Of joys, and rarefied delights;
An hundred thousand goods, glories, and graces;
    And many a mystic thing,
    Which the divine embraces
Of the dear Spouse of spirits, with them will bring;
    For which it is no shame
That dull mortality must not know a name.
    Of all this hidden store
Of blessings, and ten thousand more
    (If when He come
    He find the heart from home)

Doubtless He will unload
Himself some otherwhere,
And pour abroad
His precious sweets
On the fair soul whom first He meets.
O fair! O fortunate! O rich! O dear!
O happy and thrice-happy she,
Dear silver-breasted dove
Whoe'er she be,
Whose early love
With wingèd vows,
Makes haste to meet her morning Spouse,
And close with His immortal kisses.
Happy indeed who never misses
To improve that precious hour,
And every day
Seize her sweet prey,
All fresh and fragrant as He rises,
Dropping with a balmy shower
A delicious dew of spices;
O let the blissful heart hold fast
Her heavenly armful; she shall taste
At once ten thousand paradises;
She shall have power
To rifle and deflower
The rich and roseal [1] spring of those rare sweets,
Which with a swelling bosom there she meets:
Boundless and infinite, bottomless treasures
Of pure inebriating pleasures.
Happy proof! she shall discover
What joy, what bliss,
How many heavens at once it is
To have her God become her Lover.

[1] Sweet as a rose.

TO THE SAME

COUNSEL CONCERNING HER CHOICE

DEAR, Heaven designèd soul,
      Amongst the rest
Of suitors that besiege your maiden breast
      Why may not I
      My fortune try
And venture to speak one good word,
Not for myself, alas! but for my dearer Lord?
You have seen already in this lower sphere
Of froth and bubbles, what to look for here:
Say, gentle soul, what can you find
      But painted shapes,
      Peacocks and apes,
      Illustrious flies,
Gilded dunghills, glorious lies ;
      Goodly surmises
      And deep disguises,
Oaths of water, words of wind?
Truth bids me say 'tis time you cease to trust
Your soul to any son of dust.
'Tis time you listen to a braver love,
      Which from above
      Calls you up higher
      And bids you come
      And choose your room
Among His own fair sons of fire ;
      Where you among
      The golden throng,
That watches at His palace doors,

May pass along,
And follow those fair stars of yours;
Stars much too fair and pure to wait upon
The false smiles of a sublunary sun.
Sweet, let me prophesy that at last 't will prove
    Your wary [1] love
Lays up his purer and more precious vows,
And means them for a far more worthy Spouse
Than this World of lies can give ye:
Even for Him, with Whom nor cost,
Nor love, nor labour can be lost;
Him Who never will deceive ye.
Let not my Lord, the mighty Lover
Of souls, disdain that I discover
    The hidden art
Of His high stratagem to win your heart:
    It was His heavenly art
    Kindly to cross you
    In your mistaken love;
    That, at the next remove
    Thence, He might toss you
    And strike your troubled heart
Home to Himself, to hide it in His breast,
    The bright ambrosial nest
Of love, of life, and everlasting rest.
    Happy mistake!
That thus shall wake
Your wise soul, never to be won
Now with a love below the sun.
Your first choice fails; O when you choose again
May it not be among the sons of men!
    [1] Timorously prudent.

DESCRIPTION OF A RELIGIOUS
HOUSE AND CONDITION OF LIFE[1]

(OUT OF BARCLAY)

NO roofs of gold o'er riotous tables shining,
  Whole days and suns devour'd with endless
    dining.
No sails of Tyrian silk, proud pavements sweeping,
Nor ivory couches costlier slumber keeping;
False lights of flaring gems; tumultuous joys;
Halls full of flattering men and frisking boys;
Whate'er false shows of short and slippery good
Mix the mad sons of men in mutual blood.
But walks and unshorn woods; and souls, just so
Unforced and genuine; but not shady though.
Our lodgings hard and homely as our fare,
That chaste and cheap, as the few clothes we wear;
Those, coarse and negligent, as the natural locks
Of these loose groves; rough as th' unpolish'd rocks.
A hasty portion of prescribèd sleep;
Obedient slumbers, that can wake and weep,
And sing, and sigh, and work, and sleep again;
Still rolling a round sphere of still-returning pain.
Hands full of hearty labours; pains that pay
And prize themselves; do much, that more they
    may,

---

[1] One may call to mind in reading this poem that
Crashaw was a friend of Nicholas Ferrar, who had a
house known to cavillers as the "Protestant nunnery" at
Little Gidding during the reigns of James I. and Charles I.
This place was destroyed by the Rebels in 1646.

And work for work, not wages; let to-morrow's
New drops, wash off the sweat of this day's sorrows.
A long and daily-dying life, which breathes
A respiration of reviving deaths.
But neither are there those ignoble stings
That nip the blossom of the World's best things,
And lash Earth-labouring souls. . . .
No cruel guard of diligent cares, that keep
Crown'd woes awake, as things too wise for sleep:
But reverent discipline, and religious fear,
And soft obedience, find sweet biding here;
Silence, and sacred rest; peace, and pure joys;
Kind loves keep house, lie close, and make no noise;
And room enough for monarchs, while none swells
Beyond the kingdoms of contentful cells.
The self-rememb'ring soul sweetly recovers
Her kindred with the stars; not basely hovers
Below: but meditates her immortal way
Home to the original source of Light and intel-
    lectual day.

ON MR. GEORGE HERBERT'S BOOK, ENTITLED, *THE TEMPLE OF SACRED POEMS*

SENT TO A GENTLEWOMAN

KNOW you, fair, on what you look?
    Divinest love lies in this book:
Expecting fire from your fair eyes,
To kindle this his sacrifice.
When your hands untie these strings,
Think you've an angel by the wings;

One that gladly will be nigh,
To wait upon each morning sigh;
To flutter in the balmy air,
Of your well-perfumèd prayer.
These white plumes of his he'll lend you,
Which every day to Heaven will send you:
To take acquaintance of the sphere,
And all the smooth-faced kindred there.
    And though Herbert's name do owe [1]
    These devotions; fairest, know
    While I thus lay them on the shrine
    Of your white hand, they are mine.

A HYMN, TO THE NAME AND HONOUR OF THE ADMIRABLE SAINT TERESA:

Foundress of the Reformation of the discalced Carmelites, both men and women; a woman for angelical height of speculation, for masculine courage of performance more than a woman; who yet a child outran maturity, and durst plot a martyrdom.

Misericordias Domini in Æternum Cantabo.

THE HYMN

LOVE, thou art absolute sole lord
   Of life and death.   To prove the word
We'll now appeal to none of all
Those thy old soldiers,[2] great and tall,

[1] Own.
[2] The early Saints.   St. Teresa was born at Avila, in Spain, 1515.

8

Ripe men of martyrdom, that could reach
    down,
With strong arms, their triumphant crown;
Such as could with lusty breath,
Speak loud into the face of Death
Their great Lord's glorious Name, to none
Of those whose spacious bosoms spread a
    throne
For Love at large to fill; spare blood and
    sweat:
And see him take a private seat,
Making his mansion in the mild
And milky soul of a soft child.

    Scarce has she learnt to lisp the name
Of martyr; yet she thinks it shame
Life should so long play with that breath
Which spent can buy so brave a death.
She never undertook to know
What Death with Love should have to do;
Nor has she e'er yet understood
Why to show love, she should shed blood,
Yet though she cannot tell you why,
She can love, and she can die.

    Scarce has she blood enough to make
A guilty sword blush for her sake;
Yet has she a heart dares hope to prove
How much less strong is Death than Love.

    Be Love but there, let poor six years
Be posed with the maturest fears
Man trembles at, you straight shall find
Love knows no nonage,[1] nor the mind;
'Tis love, not years or limbs that can
Make the martyr, or the man.

            [1] Immaturity.

Love touched her heart, and lo it beats
High, and burns with such brave heats;
Such thirsts to die, as dares drink up
A thousand cold deaths in one cup.
Good reason; for she breathes all fire;
Her white breast heaves with strong desire
Of what she may, with fruitless wishes,
Seek for amongst her mother's kisses.

Since 'tis not to be had at home
She'll travel to a martyrdom.
No home for hers confesses she
But where she may a martyr be.
She'll to the Moors; and trade with them
For this unvalued diadem:
She'll offer them her dearest breath,
With Christ's name in't, in change for death:
She'll bargain with them, and will give
Them God, teach them how to live
In Him; or, if they this deny,
For Him she'll teach them how to die.
So shall she leave amongst them sown
Her Lord's blood, or at least her own.

Farewell then, all the World adieu;
Teresa is no more for you.
Farewell, all pleasures, sports, and joys
(Never till now esteemèd toys)
Farewell, whatever dear may be,
Mother's arms, or father's knee:
Farewell house, and farewell home!
She's for the Moors, and martyrdom.
 ⌐Sweet, not so fast! lo, thy fair Spouse
Whom thou seek'st with so swift vows;
Calls thee back, and bids thee come
T' embrace a milder martyrdom.⌐

Blest powers forbid, thy tender life
Should bleed upon a barbarous knife :
Or some base hand have power to rase
Thy breast's chaste cabinet, and uncase
A soul kept there so sweet : O no,
Wise Heaven will never have it so.
Thou art Love's victim ; and must die
A death more mystical and high :
Into Love's arms thou shalt let fall
A still-surviving funeral.
His is the dart must make the death
Whose stroke shall taste thy hallowed
        breath ;
A dart thrice dipp'd in that rich flame
Which writes thy Spouse's radiant Name
Upon the roof of Heaven, where aye
It shines ; and with a sovereign ray
Beats bright upon the burning faces
Of souls which in that Name's sweet
        graces
Find everlasting smiles : so rare,
So spiritual, pure, and fair
Must be th' immortal instrument
Upon whose choice point shall be sent
A life so loved : and that there be
Fit executioners for thee,
The fairest and first-born sons of fire.
Blest seraphim, shall leave their quire,
And turn Love's soldiers, upon thee
To exercise their archery.
O how oft shalt thou complain
Of a sweet and subtle pain :
Of intolerable joys :
Of a death, in which who dies

Loves his death, and dies again,
And would for ever so be slain.
And lives, and dies; and knows not why
To live, but that he thus may never leave to
 die.
How kindly will thy gentle heart
Kiss the sweetly-killing dart,
And close in his embraces keep
Those delicious wounds, that weep
Balsam to heal themselves with; thus
When these thy deaths, so numerous,
Shall all at last die into one,
And melt thy soul's sweet mansion;
Like a soft lump of incense, hasted
By too hot a fire, and wasted
Into perfuming clouds, so fast
Shalt thou exhale to Heaven at last
In a resolving sigh, and then
O what? Ask not the tongues of men;
Angels cannot tell; suffice
Thyself shalt feel thine own full joys,
And hold them fast for ever there.
So soon as thou shalt first appear,
The moon of maiden stars, thy white
Mistress, attended by such bright
Souls as thy shining self, shall come
And in her first ranks make thee room;
Where 'mongst her snowy family
Immortal welcomes wait for thee.
 O what delight, when revealed Life shall
  stand,
And teach thy lips Heaven with His hand;
On which thou now may'st to thy wishes
Heap up thy consecrated kisses.

What joys shall seize thy soul, when She,[1]
Bending her blessed eyes on Thee,
(Those second smiles of Heaven,) shall dart
Her mild rays through Thy melting heart.

Angels, thy old friends, there shall greet thee,
Glad at their own home now to meet thee.

All thy good works which went before
And waited for thee, at the door,
Shall own thee there; and all in one
Weave a constellation
Of crowns, with which the King thy Spouse
Shall build up thy triumphant brows.

All thy old woes shall now smile on thee,
And thy pains sit bright upon thee,
All thy sorrows here shall shine,
All thy sufferings be divine:
Tears shall take comfort, and turn gems,
And wrongs repent to diadems.
Even thy death shall live; and new
Dress the soul, that erst he slew.
Thy wounds shall blush to such bright scars
As keep account of the Lamb's wars.

Those rare works where thou shalt leave writ
Love's noble history, with wit [2]
Taught thee by none but Him, while here
They feed our souls, shall clothe thine there.
Each heavenly word, by whose hid flame
Our hard hearts shall strike fire, the same
Shall flourish on thy brows, and be
Both fire to us and flame to thee;
Whose light shall live bright in thy face
By glory, in our hearts by grace.

[1] The Blessed Virgin.
[2] Knowledge.

Thou shalt look round about, and see
Thousands of crown'd souls throng to be
Themselves thy crown : sons of thy vows,
The virgin-births with which thy sovereign Spouse
Made fruitful thy fair soul. Go now
And with them all about thee, bow
To Him ; put on, (He'll say,) put on
(My rosy love) that thy rich zone
Sparkling with the sacred flames
Of thousand souls, whose happy names
Heaven keep upon thy score : (Thy bright
Life brought them first to kiss the light,
That kindled them to stars,) and so
Thou with the Lamb, thy Lord, shalt go,
And wheresoe'er He sets His white
Steps, walk with Him those ways of light,
Which who in death would live to see,
Must learn in life to die like thee.

AN APOLOGY FOR THE FOREGOING HYMN

AS HAVING BEEN WRIT WHEN THE AUTHOR WAS YET AMONG THE PROTESTANTS

THUS have I back again to thy bright name,
  (Fair flood of holy fires !) transfus'd[1] the
    flame
I took from reading thee ; 'tis to thy wrong,
I know, that in my weak and worthless song
Thou here art set to shine, where thy full day
Scarce dawns.   O pardon, if I dare to say

[1] Thus have I given back the flame I took from reading thee.

Thine own dear books[1] are guilty. For from
    thence
I learn'd to know that Love is eloquence.
That hopeful maxim gave me heart to try
If, what to other tongues is tuned so high,
Thy praise might not speak English too : forbid
(By all thy mysteries that there lie hid)
Forbid it, mighty Love ! let no fond hate
Of names and words so far prejudicate.
Souls are not Spaniards too : one friendly flood
Of Baptism blends them all into a blood.
Christ's Faith makes but one body of all souls,
And Love's that body's soul ; no law controls
Our free traffic for Heaven ; we may maintain
Peace, sure, with piety, though it come from
    Spain,
What soul soe'er in any language, can
Speak Heav'n like hers, is my soul's countryman.
O 'tis not Spanish, but 'tis Heav'n she speaks,
'Tis Heav'n that lies in ambush there, and breaks
From thence into the wondering reader's breast ;
Who feels his warm heart hatch into a nest
Of little eagles and young loves, whose high
Flights scorn the lazy dust, and things that die.
There are enow whose draughts (as deep as Hell)
Drink up all Spain in sack.   Let my soul swell
With the strong wine of Love : let others swim
In puddles ; we will pledge these Seraphim [2]

---

[1] St. Teresa was a great mystical Saint. In her books
she gives Mysticism almost the appearance of an exact
science. Among her books are, her *Autobiography*, *The
Interior Castle*, *The Way of Perfection*, and *The Book of the
Foundations*.
  [2] An emblem of St. Teresa.

Bowls full of richer blood than blush of grape
Was ever guilty of.   Change we our shape,
(My soul) some drink from men to beasts, O then
Drink we till we prove more, not less than men,
And turn not beasts, but angels.   Let the King
Me ever into these His cellars bring,
Where flows such wine as we can have of none
But Him Who trod the wine-press all alone :
Wine of youth, life, and the sweet deaths of Love ;
Wine of immortal mixture ; which can prove
Its tincture from the rosy nectar ; wine
That can exalt weak earth ; and so refine
Our dust, that, at one draught, Mortality
May drink itself up, and forget to die.

✓ THE FLAMIMG HEART :

UPON THE BOOK AND PICTURE OF THE SERÁPHICAL SAINT
TERESA AS SHE IS USUALLY EXPRESSED WITH A
SERAPHIM BESIDE HER

WELL-MEANING readers, you that come
    as friends,
And catch the precious name this piece pretends ; [1]
Make not too much haste to admire
That fair-cheek'd fallacy of fire.
That is a seraphim, they say,
And this the great Teresia.
Readers, be ruled by me ; and make
Here a well-placed and wise mistake ;
You must transpose the picture quite,
And spell it wrong to read it right ;

[1] Holds out.

Read him for her, and her for him,
And call the saint the seraphim.
  Painter, what didst thou understand
To put her dart into his hand?
See, even the years and size of him
Shows this the mother-seraphim.
This is the mistress-flame; and duteous he
Her happy fire-works, here, comes down to see.
O most poor-spirited of men!
Had thy cold pencil kiss'd her pen,
Thou couldst not so unkindly err
To show us this faint shade for her.
Why, man, this speaks pure mortal frame;
And mocks with female frost Love's manly
    flame.
One would suspect thou meant'st to paint
Some weak, inferior, woman-saint.
But had thy pale-faced purple took
Fire from the burning cheeks of that bright
    book,
Thou wouldst on her have heap'd up all
That could be found seraphical;
Whate'er this youth of fire wears fair,
Rosy fingers, radiant hair,
Glowing cheek, and glist'ring wings,
All those fair and fragrant things,
But before all, that fiery dart
Had fill'd the hand of this great heart.
  Do then, as equal right requires;
Since his the blushes be, and hers the fires,
Resume and rectify thy rude design;
Undress thy seraphim into mine;
Redeem this injury of thy art,
Give him the veil, give her the dart.

Give him the veil, that he may cover
The red cheeks of a rivall'd lover;
Ashamed that our world now can show
Nests of new seraphim here below.
   Give her the dart, for it is she
(Fair youth) shoots both thy shaft and thee;
Say, all ye wise and well-pierced hearts
That live and die amidst her darts,
What is't your tasteful spirits do prove
In that rare life of her, and Love?
Say, and bear witness. Sends she not
A seraphim at every shot?
What magazines of immortal arms there shine!
Heaven's great artillery in each love-spun line.
Give then the dart to her who gives the flame;
Give him the veil, who gives the shame.
   But if it be the frequent fate
Of worse-faults to be fortunate;
If all's prescription; and proud wrong
Hearkens not to an humble song;
For all the gallantry of him,
Give me the suffering seraphim.
His be the bravery of all those bright things,
The glowing cheeks, the glistering wings;
The rosy hand, the radiant dart;
Leave her alone the flaming heart.
   Leave her that; and thou shalt leave her
Not one loose shaft, but Love's whole quiver;
For in Love's field was never found
A nobler weapon than a wound.
Love's passives are his activ'st part:
The wounded is the wounding heart.
O heart! the equal poise of Love's both parts,
Big alike with wound and darts,

Live in these conquering leaves; live all the same;
And walk through all tongues one triumphant
flame.
Live here, great heart; and love, and die, and kill;
And bleed, and wound; and yield and conquer
still.
Let this immortal life where'er it comes
Walk in a crowd of loves and martyrdoms.
Let mystic deaths wait on't; and wise souls be
The love-slain witnesses of this life of thee.
  O sweet incendiary! show here thy art,
Upon this carcass of a hard cold heart;
Let all thy scatter'd shafts of light that play
Among the leaves of thy large books of day,
Combined against this breast at once break in
And take away from me myself and sin;
This gracious robbery shall thy bounty be,
And my best fortunes such fair spoils of me.
O thou undaunted daughter of desires!
By all thy dower of lights and fires;
By all the eagle in thee, all the dove;
By all thy lives and deaths of love;
By thy large draughts of intellectual day,
And by thy thirsts of love more large than they;
By all thy brim-fill'd bowls of fierce desire,
By thy last morning's draught of liquid fire;
By the full kingdom of that final kiss
That seized thy parting soul, and seal'd thee His;
By all the Heaven thou hast in Him
(Fair sister of the seraphim!)
By all of Him we have in thee;
Leave nothing of myself in me.
Let me so read thy life, that I
Unto all life of mine may die.

A SONG OF DIVINE LOVE

LORD, when the sense of Thy sweet grace
    Sends up my soul to seek Thy face,
Thy blessed eyes breed such desire,
I die in Love's delicious fire.
    O Love, I am thy sacrifice ;
Be still triumphant, blessed eyes ;
Still shine on me, fair suns, that I
Still may behold, though still I die.

Though still I die, I live again ;
Still longing so to be still slain ;
So gainful is such loss of breath ;
I die even in desire of death.
    Still live in me this loving strife
Of living death and dying life ;
For while Thou sweetly slayest me
Dead to myself, I live in Thee.

IN THE GLORIOUS ASSUMPTION OF OUR BLESSED LADY

THE HYMN

HARK ! she is call'd, the parting hour is come;
    Take thy farewell, poor World, Heaven
    must go home.
A piece of heavenly earth, purer and brighter
Than the chaste stars whose choice lamps come to
    light her,
Whilst through the crystal orbs clearer than they
She climbs, and makes a far more Milky Way.

She's call'd ! Hark, how the dear immortal Dove
Sighs to His silver mate: " Rise up, my love ! "
Rise up, my fair, my spotless one,
The Winter's past, the rain is gone,
The Spring is come, the flowers appear,
No sweets (save thou) are wanting here.
  Come away, my love,
  Come away, my dove,
      Cast off delay ;
    The court of Heaven is come
    To wait upon thee home ;
      Come, come away.

The flowers appear,
Or quickly would, wert thou once here.
The Spring is come, or if it stay
'Tis to keep time with thy delay.
The rain is gone, except so much as we,
Detain in needful tears to weep the want of thee.
      The Winter's past,
      Or if he make less haste
His answer is why she does so,
If Summer come not, how can Winter go ?
      Come away, come away !
The shrill winds chide, the waters weep thy stay ;
The fountains murmur, and each loftiest tree
Bows lowest his leafy top, to look for thee.
      Come away, my love,
      Come away, my dove, etc.

She's call'd again. And will she go ?
When Heaven bids come, who can say no ?
Heaven calls her, and she must away,
Heaven will not, and she cannot, stay.

Go then, go glorious on the golden wings
Of the bright youth of Heaven, that sings
Under so sweet a burthen.   Go,
Since thy dread Son will have it so :
And while thou go'st, our song and we
Will, as we may, reach after thee.
Hail, Holy Queen of humble hearts,
We in thy praise will have our parts.
And though thy dearest looks must now give light
To none but the blest heavens, whose bright
Beholders, lost in sweet delight,
Feed for ever their fair sight
With those divinest eyes, which we
And our dark world no more shall see ;
Though our poor eyes are parted so,
Yet shall our lips never let go
Thy gracious Name, but to the last,
Our loving song shall hold it fast.
       Thy precious Name shall be
       Thyself to us ; and we
          With holy care will keep it by us,
          We to the last
          Will hold it fast,
        And no Assumption shall deny us.
       All the sweetest showers
       Of our fairest flowers
       Will we strow upon it.
       Though our sweets cannot make
       It sweeter, they can take
       Themselves new sweetness from it.
Maria, men and angels sing,
Maria, Mother of our King.
Live, rosy Princess, live, and may the bright
Crown of a most incomparable light

Embrace thy radiant brows.   O may the best
Of everlasting joys bathe thy white breast.
Live, our chaste love, the holy mirth
Of Heaven ; the humble pride of Earth.
Live, crown of women, queen of men,
Live, mistress of our song ; and when
Our weak desires have done their best,
Sweet angels come, and sing the rest.

ON A TREATISE OF CHARITY [1]

RISE, then, immortal maid, Religion, rise !
    Put on thyself in thine own looks : t' our eyes
Be what thy beauties, not our blots, have made thee,
Such as (ere our dark sins to dust betray'd thee)
Heaven set thee down new dress'd ; when thy bright
    birth
Shot thee like lightning to th' astonished Earth.
From th' dawn of thy fair eyelids wipe away
Dull mists and melancholy clouds : take Day
And thine own beams about thee : bring the best
Of whatsoe'er perfumed thy Eastern nest,
Girt all thy glories to thee ; then sit down,
Open this book, fair Queen, and take thy crown.
These learnèd leaves shall vindicate to thee
Thy holiest, humblest handmaid, Charity.
She'll dress thee like thyself, set thee on high
Where thou shalt reach all hearts, command each eye.
Lo ! where I see thy offerings wake, and rise
From the pale dust of that strange sacrifice
Which they themselves were ; each one putting on
A majesty that may beseem thy throne.

[1] The treatise *On Charity*, on which Crashaw has
written this poem, was by Robert Shelford, parson of
Ringsfield, in Suffolk.

The holy youth of Heaven, whose golden rings
Girt round thy awful altars, with bright wings
Fanning thy fair locks (which the World believes
As much as sees) shall with these sacred leaves
Trick their tall plumes, and in that garb shall go
If not more glorious, more conspicuous though.
————Be it enacted then
By the fair laws of thy firm-pointed pen,
God's services no longer shall put on
Pure sluttishness for pure religion:
No longer shall our Churches' frighted stones
Lie scatter'd like the burnt and martyr'd bones
Of dead Devotion, nor faint marbles weep
In their sad ruins, nor Religion keep
A melancholy mansion in those cold
Urns. Like God's sanctuaries they look'd of
    old:
Now seem they Temples consecrate to none,
Or to a new god, Desolation.[1]
No more the hypocrite shall th' upright be
Because he's stiff, and will confess no knee:
While others bend their knee, no more shalt thou,
(Disdainful dust and ashes) bend thy brow;
Nor on God's altar cast two scorching eyes
Baked in hot scorn, for a burnt sacrifice:
But (for a lamb) thy tame and tender heart
New struck by Love, still trembling on his dart;
Or (for two turtle-doves) it shall suffice
To bring a pair of meek and humble eyes.
This shall from henceforth be the masculine theme
Pulpits and pens shall sweat in; to redeem

[1] Peterhouse Chapel was terribly handled by the Rebels.
Crashaw used to be fond of praying there when he was
a Fellow.

9

Virtue to action, that life-feeding flame
That keeps Religion warm : not swell a name
Of Faith ; a mountain-word, made up of air,
With those dear spoils that wont to dress the fair
And fruitful Charity's full breasts (of old),
Turning her out to tremble in the cold.
What can the poor·hope from us, when we be
Uncharitable even to Charity ?
Nor shall our zealous ones [1] still have a fling
At that most horrible and hornèd thing,
Forsooth the Pope : by which black name they call
The Turk, the·devil, Furies, Hell and all,
And something more.[2] O he is Anti-Christ :
Doubt this and doubt (say they) that Christ is Christ :
Why, 'tis a point of Faith. Whate'er it be,
I'm sure it is no point of Charity.
In sum, no longer shall our people hope,
To be a true Protestant's but to hate the Pope.

DIES IRÆ, DIES ILLA

THE HYMN OF THE CHURCH, IN MEDITATION OF THE DAY OF JUDGMENT

I

H EAR'ST thou, my soul, what serious things
Both the Psalm and Sibyl [3] sings

[1] Evidently the Puritan party.
[2] Crashaw's friend Shelford, author of this Treatise on which he is writing, was an Anglican priest, and had repudiated the idea of the Pope being Anti-Christ dear to the Puritan mind.
[3] Dies iræ, dies illa
Solvet sæclum in favilla
Teste David cum Sibylla, etc.

Of a sure Judge, from Whose sharp ray
The World in flames shall fly away.

II

'O that fire, before whose face
Heaven and Earth shall find no place.
O those eyes, Whose angry light
Must be the day of that dread night.

III

O that trump, whose blast shall run
An even round with the circling sun,
And urge the murmuring graves to bring
Pale mankind forth to meet his King.

IV

Horror of Nature, Hell, and Death,
When a deep groan from beneath
Shall cry, "We come, we come," and all
The caves of Night answer one call.

V

O that Book,[1] whose leaves so bright
Will set the World in severe light.
O that Judge, Whose hand, Whose eye
None can endure; yet none can fly.

VI

Ah then, poor soul, what wilt thou say?
And to what patron[2] choose to pray?

[1] Liber scriptus proferetur
In quo totum continetur
Unde mundus judicetur.
[2] Quem patronum rogaturus.

When stars themselves shall stagger, and
The most firm foot no more then stand.

VII

But Thou givest leave (dread Lord!) that we
Take shelter from Thyself in Thee;
And with the wings of Thine Own Dove
Fly to Thy sceptre of soft love.

VIII [1]

Dear, remember in that Day
Who was the cause Thou cam'st this way.
Thy sheep was stray'd; and Thou would'st be
Even lost Thyself in seeking me.

IX

Shall all that labour, all that cost
Of love, and even that loss, be lost?
And this loved soul, judged worth no less
Than all that way and weariness?

X

Just mercy, then, Thy reck'ning be
With my Price, and not with me;
'Twas paid at first with too much pain,
To be paid twice, or once, in vain.

XI

Mercy (my Judge), mercy I cry
With blushing cheek and bleeding eye:
The conscious colours of my sin
Are red without and pale within.

[1] Recordare Jesu pie,
Quod sum causa tuæ viæ,
Ne me perdas illa die.

XII

O let Thine Own soft bowels pay
Thyself, and so discharge that day.
If Sin can sigh, Love can forgive :
O say the word, my soul shall live !

XIII [1]

Those mercies which Thy Mary found,
Or who Thy cross confess'd and crown'd,
Hope tells my heart, the same loves be
Still alive, and still for me.

XIV [2]

Though both my prayers and tears combine,
Both worthless are ; for they are mine.
But Thou Thy bounteous Self still be ;
And show Thou art, by saving me.

XV [3]

O when Thy last frown shall proclaim
The flocks of goats to folds of flame,
And all Thy lost sheep found shall be ;
Let, " Come, ye blessed," then call me.

[1] Qui Mariam absolvísti,
Et latronem exaudisti,
Mihi quoque spem dedisti.
[2] Preces meæ non sunt dignæ.
Sed tu bonus fac benigne,
Ne perenni cremer igne.
[3] Confutatis maledictis,
Flammis acribus addictis,
Voca me cum benedictis.

XVI

When the dread " *Ite* " [1] shall divide
Those limbs of death from Thy left side;
Let those life-speaking lips command
That I inherit Thy right hand.

XVII [2]

O' hear a suppliant heart, all crushed
And crumbled into contrite dust.
My Hope, my Fear, my Judge, my Friend,
Take charge of me, and of my end.

CHARITAS NIMIA,
OR, THE DEAR BARGAIN

LORD, what is man? why should he cost Thee
So dear? what had his ruin lost Thee?
Lord, what is man, that thou hast over-bought
So much a thing of nought?

Love is too kind, I see; and can
Make but a simple merchant-man.
'Twas for such sorry merchandise
Bold painters have put out his eyes.

Alas, sweet Lord, what were't to Thee
If there were no such worms as we?

[1] Go ye.
[2] Oro supplex et acclinis
    Cor contritum quasi cinis
    Gere curam mei finis.

Heaven ne'ertheless still Heaven would be,
    Should mankind dwell
    In the deep Hell :
What have his woes to do with Thee ?

    Let him go weep
    O'er his own wounds ;
    Seraphim will not sleep,
Nor spheres let fall their faithful rounds.

    Still would the youthful spirits sing ;
And still Thy spacious palace ring ;
Still would those beauteous ministers of light
    Burn all as bright,
And bow their flaming heads before Thee ;
Still thrones and dominations would adore Thee ;
Still would those ever-wakeful sons of fire [1]
    Keep warm Thy praise
    Both nights and days,
And teach Thy loved name to their noble lyre.

Let froward dust then do its kind ;
And give itself for sport to the proud wind.
Why should a piece of peevish clay plead shares
In the eternity of Thy old cares ?
Why should'st Thou bow Thy awful breast to see
What mine own madnesses have done with me ?

Should not the king still keep his throne
Because some desperate fool's undone ?
Or will the World's illustrious eyes
Weep for every worm that dies ?

[1] Job xxxviii. 7 : " The morning stars sang together,
and all the sons of God shouted for joy."

Will the gallant sun
E'er the less glorious run?
Will he hang down his golden head,
Or e'er the sooner seek his Western bed,
Because some foolish fly
Grows wanton, and will die?

If I were lost in misery,
What was it to Thy Heaven and Thee?
What was it to Thy Precious Blood,
If my foul heart call'd for a flood?
What if my faithless soul and I
Would needs fall in
With guilt and sin;
What did the Lamb that He should die?
What did the Lamb that He should need,
When the wolf sins, Himself to bleed?

If my base lust
Bargain'd with Death and well-beseeming dust:
Why should the white
Lamb's bosom write
The purple name
Of my sin's shame?
Why should His unstain'd breast make good
My blushes with His Own heart-blood?

O my Saviour, make me see
How dearly Thou hast paid for me;
That lost again, my life may prove,
As then in death, so now in love.

ST. MARIA MAJOR

Dilectus meus mihi, et ego illi, qui pascitur inter lilia.
—CANT. vi. 3.

THE HYMN, O GLORIOSA DOMINA

HAIL, most high, most humble one!
　　Above the world, below thy Son;
Whose blush the moon beauteously mars,
And stains the timorous light of stars.
He that made all things had not done
Till He had made Himself thy Son.
The whole World's host would be thy guest,
And board Himself at thy rich breast.
O boundless hospitality!
The Feast of all things feeds on thee.
　　The first Eve, mother of our Fall,
Ere she bore any one, slew all.[1]
Of her unkind gift might we have
Th' inheritance of a hasty grave:
Quick buried in the wanton tomb
　　　　Of one forbidden bit,
Had not a better fruit forbidden it.
　　　　Had not thy healthful womb
　　The World's new eastern window been,
And given us heaven again in giving Him.
Thine was the rosy dawn that sprung the day,
Which renders all the stars she stole away.
　　Let then the agèd World be wise, and all
Prove nobly here unnatural:
'Tis gratitude to forget that other,
And call the maiden Eve their mother.
　　　　　[1] Gen. iii. 19.

Ye redeem'd nations far and near,
Applaud your happy selves in her ;
(All you to whom this love belongs)
And keep't alive with lasting songs.
  Let hearts and lips speak loud and say,
Hail, door of life, and source of Day !
The door was shut, the fountain seal'd,
Yet Light was seen and Life reveal'd.
The door was shut, yet let in day,
The fountain seal'd, yet life found way.
  Glory to Thee, great virgin's Son,
In bosom of Thy Father's bliss.
  The same to Thee, sweet Spirit, be done ;
As ever shall be, was, and is.   Amen.

AGAINST IRRESOLUTION AND
DELAY IN MATTERS OF RELIGION [1]

TO THE COUNTESS DENBIGH

WHAT Heaven-besiegèd heart is this
      Stands trembling at the Gate of Bliss :
Holds fast the door, yet dares not venture
Fairly [2] to open and to enter ?
Whose definition is A Doubt
'Twixt life and death, 'twixt In and Out.
Ah ! linger not, loved soul : a slow
And late consent was a long No ;
Who grants at last, a great while tried
And did his best, to have denied.
What magic-bolts, what mystic bars
Maintain the Will in these strange wars ?

---

[1] 1653 version.   [2] To open wide.

What fatal, yet fantastic, bands
Keep the free heart from his own hands?
Say, lingering Fair, why comes the birth
Of your brave soul so slowly forth?
Plead your pretences (O you strong
In weakness) why you choose so long
In labour of yourself to lie,
Not daring quite to live nor die.

So when the Year takes cold we see
Poor waters their own prisoners be:
Fetter'd and lock'd up fast they lie
In a cold self-captivity.
Th' astonish'd Nymphs their Flood's strange fate
       deplore
To find themselves their own severer shore.

Love, that lends haste to heaviest things,
In you alone hath lost his wings.
Look round and read the World's wide face,
The field of Nature or of Grace;
Where can you fix, to find excuse
Or pattern for the pace you use?
Mark with what faith fruits answer flowers,
And know the call of Heaven's kind showers:
Each mindful plant hastes to make good
The hope and promise of his bud.
Seed-time's not all: there should be harvest
       too.
Alas! and has the Year no Spring for you?
Both winds and waters urge their way,
And murmur if they meet a stay.
Mark how the curled waves work and wind,
All hating to be left behind.
Each big with business thrusts the other,
And seems to say: " Make haste, my brother "

The aëry nation of neat doves,
That draw the chariot of chaste Loves,
Chide your delay : yea, those dull things,
Whose ways have least to do with wings,
Make wings, at least, of their own weight,
And by their love control their fate.
So lumpish steel, untaught to move,
Learn'd first his lightness by his love.

　Whate'er love's matter be, he moves
By th' even wings of his own doves,
Lives by his own laws, and does hold
In grossest metals his own gold.

　All things swear friends to Fair and Good,
Yea suitors : man alone is wooed,
Tediously wooed, and hardly won,
Only not slow to be undone ;
As if the bargain had been driven
So hardly betwixt Earth and Heaven,
Our God would thrive too fast, and be
Too much a gainer by 't, should we
Our purchased selves too soon bestow
On Him, who has not loved us so.
When love of us called Him to see
If we'd vouchsafe His company,
He left His Father's Court, and came
Lightly as a lambent[1] flame,
Leaping upon the hills, to be
The humble King of you and me.
Nor can the cares of His whole crown
(When one poor sigh sends for Him down)
Detain Him, but He leaves behind
The late wings of the lazy wind,
　Spurns the tame laws of Time and Place,

[1] Playing about, gliding over.

And breaks thro' all ten heavens [1] to our embrace.
 Yield to his siege, wise soul, and see
Your triumph in His victory.
Disband dull fears, give Faith the day:
To save your life, kill your Delay.
'Tis cowardice that keeps this field;
And want of courage not to yield.
 Yield then, O yield, that Love may win
The Fort at last, and let Life in.
Yield quickly, lest perhaps you prove
Death's prey before the prize of Love.
This fort of your fair self, if 't be not won,
He is repulsed indeed; but you're undone.

TO THE NOBLEST AND BEST OF LADIES, THE COUNTESS OF DENBIGH [2]

PERSUADING HER TO RESOLUTION IN RELIGION, AND TO RENDER HERSELF WITHOUT FURTHER DELAY INTO THE COMMUNION OF THE CATHOLIC CHURCH

WHAT Heaven-entreated heart is this,
 Stands trembling at the gate of bliss?
Holds fast the door, yet dares not venture
Fairly to open it, and enter;

[1] I know not where Crashaw got his idea of ten heavens from. According to the Jewish system there were three. The Ptolemaic said five, the Mahometan seven, and the late Latin poets say nine. But ten we know not.

[2] This is another poem to the same lady. Clearly only a version of the preceding.

Whose definition is a doubt
'Twixt Life and Death, 'twixt In and Out.
Say, ling'ring Fair! why comes the birth
Of your brave soul so slowly forth?
Plead your pretences (O you strong
In weakness!) why you choose so long
In labour of yourself to lie,
Nor daring quite to live nor die.
Ah! linger not, loved soul, a slow
And late consent was a long No;
Who grants at last, long time tried
And did his best to have denied:
What magic bolts, what mystic bars,
Maintain the will in these strange wars?
What fatal yet fantastic bands
Keep the free heart from its own hands?
So when the year takes cold, we see
Poor waters their own prisoners be,
Fettered, and lockèd up they lie
In a sad self-captivity.
The astonish'd Nymphs their flood's strange fate
  deplore,
To see themselves their own severer shore.
Thou that alone canst thaw this cold,
And fetch the heart from its stronghold,
Almighty Love! end this long war,
And of a meteor make a star.
O fix this fair Indefinite!
And 'mongst Thy shafts of sov'reign light
Choose out that sure decisive dart
Which has the key of this close heart,
Knows all the corners of't, and can control
The self-shut cabinet of an unsearch'd soul.
O let it be at last, Love's hour;

Raise this tall trophy of Thy power;
Come once the conquering way; not to confute
But kill this rebel-word "irresolute,"
That so, in spite of all this peevish strength
Of weakness, she may write "resolved" at
    length.
Unfold at length, unfold fair flower,
And use the season of Love's shower!
Meet his well-meaning wounds, wise heart!
And haste to drink the wholesome dart.
That healing shaft, which Heaven till now
Hath in love's quiver hid for you.
O dart of Love! arrow of light!
O happy you, if it hit right!
It must not fall in vain, it must
Not mark the dry regardless dust.
Fair one, it is your fate; and brings
Eternal words upon its wings.
Meet it with wide-spread arms, and see
Its seat your soul's just centre be.
Disband dull fears, give faith the day;
To save your life, kill your delay.
It is Love's siege, and sure to be
Your triumph, though His victory.
'Tis cowardice that keeps this field,
And want of courage not to yield.
Yield then, O yield, that Love may win
The fort at last, and let life in.
Yield quickly, lest perhaps you prove
Death's prey, before the prize of Love.
This fort of your fair self, if 't be not won,
He is repulsed indeed, but you're undone.

DIVINE EPIGRAMS

" Two went up into the Temple to pray."

TWO went to pray!   O, rather say
    One went to brag, th' other to pray ;
One stands up close and treads on high,
Where th' other dares not send his eye.
One nearer to God's altar trod,
The other to the altar's God.

Upon the ass that bore our Saviour.

HATH only Anger an omnipotence [1]
            In eloquence ?
Within the lips of Love and Joy doth dwell
            No miracle ?
Why else had Balaam's ass a tongue to chide
            His master's pride,
And thou (Heaven-burthen'd beast) hast ne'er a
    word
            To praise thy Lord ?
That he should find a tongue and vocal thunder,
            Was a great wonder ;
But O, methinks, 'tis a far greater one
            That thou find'st none.

On the Proaigal.—LUKE xv.

TELL me, bright boy, tell me, my golden lad,
Whither away so frolic ? [2] why so glad ?
What all thy wealth in council ? all thy state ?
Are husks so dear ? troth, 'tis a mighty rate.

[1] Num. xxii. 28.   [2] Gay.

On St. Peter casting away his nets at our Saviour's call.

THOU hast the art on't, Peter, and canst tell
To cast thy nets on all occasions well.
When Christ calls, and thy nets would have thee
    stay,
To cast them well's to cast them quite away.

Upon Lazarus's tears.

RICH Lazarus! richer in those gems, thy tears,
Than Dives in the robes he wears:
He scorns them now, but O! they'll suit full well
With th' purple he must wear in Hell.

Dives asks a drop.—LUKE xvi. 24.

A DROP, one drop, how sweetly one fair drop
Would tremble on my pearl-tipp'd finger's top!
My wealth is gone; O! go it where it will,
Spare this one jewel; I'll be Dives still.

On the Miracle of Loaves.

Now, Lord, or never, they'll believe on Thee;
Thou to their teeth hast proved Thy Deity.

On the Miracle of Multiplied Loaves.

SEE here an easy feast that knows no wound,
That under Hunger's teeth will needs be found:
A subtle harvest of unbounded bread;
What would ye more? Here food itself is fed,

10

The blind cured by the word of our Saviour.—
MATT. X.

THOU spak'st the word (Thy word's a law)
Thou spak'st, and straight the blind man saw.
To speak and make the blind man see,
"Was never man, Lord, spake like Thee."
To speak thus, was to speak (say I)
Not to his ear, but to his eye.

The widow's mites.—LUKE xxi. 2, 3.

Two mites, two drops (yet all her house and land)
Fall from a steady heart, though trembling hand:
The other's wanton wealth foams high and brave.
The other cast away; she only gave.

" And He answered nothing."—MATT. xxvii. 12.

O MIGHTY Nothing! unto thee,
Nothing, we owe all things that be;
God spake once when He all things made,
He saved all when He Nothing said.
The world was made of Nothing then;
'Tis made by Nothing now again.

*" I am not worthy that Thou shouldest come under
my roof."*—MATT. viii. 8.

THY God was making haste into thy roof,
Thy humble faith and fear keeps Him aloof:
He'll be thy guest, because He may not be;
He'll come—into thy house? No, into thee.

To our Lord, upon the water made wine.

THOU water turn'st to wine (fair friend of life);
   Thy foe, to cross the sweet acts of Thy reign,
Distils from thence the tears of wrath and strife,
   And so turns wine to water back again.

"It is better to go into Heaven with one eye," etc.
       — MARK ix. 47.

ONE eye? a thousand rather, and a thousand more,
To fix those full-faced glories! O, he's poor
Of eyes that has but Argus' [1] store.
Yet, if thou'lt fill one poor eye with Thy Heaven
    and Thee,
O grant, sweet Goodness, that one eye may be
All and every whit of me.

"But now they have seen and hated."—
      JOHN xv. 24.

SEEN? and yet hated Thee? they did not see,
They saw Thee not, that saw and hated Thee:
No, no, they saw Thee not, O Life, O Love,
Who saw aught in Thee that their hate could
    move!

On the water of our Lord's Baptism.

    EACH blest drop on each blest limb
    Is wash'd itself in washing Him:
    'Tis a gem while it stays here;
    While it falls hence 'tis a tear.

[1] A son of Jupiter having a hundred eyes and so called
the "all seeing."

" Give to Cæsar—and to God."—MARK xii. 17.

ALL we have is God's, and yet
Cæsar challenges a debt ;
Nor hath God a thinner [1] share,
Whatever Cæsar's payments are.
All is God's ; and yet 'tis true
All we have is Cæsar's too.
All is Cæsar's : and what odds,
So long as Cæsar's self is God's ?

On the Blessed Virgin's bashfulness.

THAT on her lap she casts her humble eye,
'Tis the sweet pride of her humility.
The fair star [2] is well fix'd, for where, O, where,
Could she have fix'd it on a fairer sphere ?
'Tis Heaven, 'tis Heaven she sees, Heaven's God
        there lies ;
She can see Heaven, and ne'er lift up her eyes.
This new guest to her eyes new laws hath given :
'Twas once look up, 'tis now look down to Heaven.

" I am ready not only to be bound but to die."— ACTS xxi. 13.

COME death, come bonds, nor do you shrink, my ears,
At those hard words man's cowardice calls fears.
Save those of fear, no other bands fear I ;
Nor other death than this—the fear to die.

" I am the Door."

AND now thou'rt set wide ope, the spear's sad art, [3]
Lo ! hath unlock'd Thee at the very heart :

[1] Smaller, lesser.   [2] Stella Maris.
[3] The spear that pierced Him.

He to himself (I fear the worst)
  And his own hope
Hath shut these doors of Heaven, that durst
  Thus set them ope.

To the infant Martyrs.

Go, smiling souls, your new-built cages break,
In Heaven you'll learn to sing ere here to speak :
Nor let the milky fonts, that bathe your thirst,
    Be your delay ;
The place that calls you hence is, at the worst,
    Milk all the way.

Upon the infant Martyrs.

To see both blended in one flood,
The mother's milk, the children's blood,
Makes me doubt if Heaven will gather
Roses hence, or lilies rather.

Upon our Lord's last comfortable discourse with His disciples.—JOHN xiv.

ALL Hybla's honey, all that sweetness can
Flows in Thy song (O fair, O dying Swan !)
Yet is the joy I take in't small or none ;
It is too sweet to be a long-lived one.

Upon the dumb devil cast out, and the slanderous Jews put to silence.—LUKE xi. 14.

Two devils at one blow Thou hast laid flat,
A speaking devil this, a dumb one that ;
Was't Thy full victory's fairer increase,
That th' one spake, or that th' other held his peace ?

The dumb healed, and the people enjoined silence.
—MARK vii. 31–37.

CHRIST bids the dumb tongue speak; it speaks, the
    sound
He charges to be quiet; it runs round.
If in the first He used His finger's touch,
His hand's whole strength here could not be too
    much.

" *She began to wash His feet with tears, and wipe
them with the hairs of her head.*"—LUKE vii. 38.

    HER eyes' flood licks His feet's fair stain,
    Her hair's flame [1] licks up that again;
    This flame thus quench'd hath brighter beams:
    This flood thus stainèd fairer streams.

" *And a certain priest coming that way looked on him
and passed by.*"—LUKE x. 31.

WHY dost thou wound my wounds, O thou that
    passest by,
Handling and turning them with an unwounded eye?
The calm that cools thine eye does shipwreck
    mine, for O,
Unmoved to see one wretched, is to make him so.

" *Verily I say unto you, ye shall weep and lament.*"
—JOHN xvi. 20.

    WELCOME, my grief, my joy; how dear's
    To me my legacy of tears!

[1] The golden hair of the Magdalene, which is often
represented too as of flame-colour.

I'll weep, and weep, and will therefore
Weep, 'cause I can weep no more:
Thou, Thou (dear Lord) even Thou alone,
Giv'st joy, even when Thou givest none.

" Ye build the sepulchres of the prophets."—
MATT. xxiii. 29.

THOU trimm'st a Prophet's tomb, and dost bequeath
The life thou took'st from him unto his death.
Vain man, the stones that on his tomb do lie,
Keep but the score of them that made him die.

On the baptized Ethiopian.—ACTS viii. 27–38.

LET it no longer be a forlorn-hope
                    To wash an Ethiop;
He's wash'd, his gloomy skin a peaceful shade
                    For his white soul is made:
And now, I doubt not, the Eternal Dove
                    A black-faced house [1] will love.

" But men loved darkness rather than light."—
JOHN iii. 19.

THE world's Light shines; shine as it will,
The world will love its darkness still.
I doubt though, when the world's in hell,
It will not love its darkness half so well.

[1] 1 Cor. vi. 19.

On St. Peter cutting off Malchus' ear.

WELL, Peter, dost thou wield thy active sword;
Well for thyself (I mean), not for thy Lord.
To strike at ears, is to take heed there be
No witness, Peter, of thy perjury.

To Pontius washing his hands.

THY hands are washed, but O, the water's spilt,
That laboured to have washed thy guilt:
The flood, if any be that can suffice,
Must have its fountain in thine eyes.

To Pontius washing his blood-stained hands.

Is murder no sin? or a sin so cheap,
    That thou need'st heap
A rape upon't? Till thy adult'rous touch
 Taught her [1] these sullied cheeks, this blubber'd
  face,
She was a nymph, the meadows knew none such,
 Of honest parentage, of unstain'd race;
The daughter of a fair and well-famed fountain,
As ever silver-tipp'd the side of shady mountain.

See how she weeps, and weeps, that she appears
    Nothing but tears;
Each drop's a tear that weeps for her own waste.
 Hark how at every touch she does complain her;
Hark how she bids her frighted drops make haste,
 And with sad murmurs chides the hands that
  stain her.
Leave, leave, for shame, or else, good judge, decree
What water shall wash this, when this hath washèd
  thee.

    [1] The water.

" Come see the place where the Lord lay."—
MATT. xxviii. 6.

SHOW me Himself, Himself (bright Sir), O show
Which way my poor tears to Himself may go :
Were it enough to show the place, and say,
Look, Mary, here, see where thy Lord once lay,
Then could I show these arms of mine, and say,
Look, Mary, here, see where thy Lord once lay.

The sick implore St. Peter's shadow.—ACTS v.

UNDER thy shadow may 1 lurk awhile,
Death's busy search I'll easily beguile :
Thy shadow, Peter, must show me the Sun,
My light's thy shadow's shadow, or 'tis done.

Samson to his Delilah.

COULD not once blinding me, cruel, suffice ?
When first I look'd on thee I lost mine eyes.

Upon the Powder Day.

How fit our well-rank'd feasts do follow,
All mischief comes after All-Hallow.[1]

Life for Death.

So I may gain Thy death my life I'll give,
My life's Thy death and in Thy death I live ;
Or else my life I'll hide thee in His grave
By three days' loss eternally to save.

[1] All Hallows Day, 1st November.

On the Divine Love.

ETERNAL Love! what 'tis to love Thee well
None but himself who feels it, none can tell.
But oh! what to be loved of Thee as well
None but himself who feels it, none can tell.

Upon the Holy Sepulchre.

HERE, where our Lord once laid His head,
Now the grave lies buried.

To our Blessed Lord upon the choice of His Sepulchre.

How life and death in Thee
　　　　　Agree.
Thou hadst a virgin womb,
　　　　　And tomb.
A Joseph [1] did betroth
　　　　　Them both.

*Upon the crown of thorns taken down from the
head of our Blessed Lord all bloody.*

KNOW'ST thou this, Soldier? 'tis a much changed
plant, which yet
　　　　　Thyself didst set,
'Tis changed indeed; did Autumn e'er such
beauties bring
　　　　　To shame his Spring?
Oh! who so hard a husbandman could ever find
　　　　　A soil so kind?
Is not the soil a kind one (think ye) that returns
　　　　　Roses for thorns?

[1] St. Joseph the affianced husband of the Blessed Virgin
and St. Joseph of Arimathea who buried our Lord in
his own tomb.

Upon the body of our Blessed Lord naked
and bloody.

THEY have left Thee naked, Lord; O that they
    had.
    This garment too I would they had denied.
Thee with Thyself they have too richly clad;
    Opening the purple wardrobe in Thy side.
O never could there be garment too good
For Thee to wear, but this of Thine own blood.

" Why are ye afraid, O ye of little faith ? "—
        MARK iv. 40.

        As if the storm meant Him;
        Or 'cause Heaven's face is dim,
           His needs a cloud.
        Was ever forward wind
        That could be so unkind,
           Or wave so proud?
The wind had need be angry, and the water black,
That to the mighty Neptune's Self dare threaten
    wrack.

        There is no storm but this
        Of your own cowardice
           That braves you out;
        You are the storm that mocks
        Yourselves; you are the rocks
           Of your own doubt:
Besides this fear of danger, there's no danger here;
And he that here fears danger, does deserve his
    fear.

On the still surviving marks of our Saviour's wounds.

WHATEVER story of their cruelty,
Or nail, or thorn, or spear have writ in Thee,
  Are in another sense
   Still legible ;
  Sweet is the difference :
   Once I did spell
  Every red letter
   A wound of Thine ;
  Now, what is better,
   Balsam for mine.

THE
DELIGHTS
OF THE
MUSES
OR,

Other Poems written on several occasions

By Richard Crashaw *sometimes* of Pembroke *Hall and late Fellow of* S*t* Peters *Colledge in* Cambridge

Mart. Dic mihi quid melius desidiosus agas

LONDON
Printed by *T. W.* for *H. Moseley*, at
the Princes Armes in S. *Pauls*
Church-yard, 1648.

MUSIC'S DUEL

NOW westward Sol had spent the richest beams
    Of Noon's high glory, when, hard by the
       streams
Of Tiber, on the scene of a green plat,
Under protection of an oak, there sat
A sweet lute's-master, in whose gentle airs
He lost the day's heat, and his own hot cares.
    Close in the covert of the leaves there stood
A Nightingale, come from the neighbouring wood,
(The sweet inhabitant of each glad tree,
Their Muse, their Syren—harmless Syren she,)
There stood she list'ning, and did entertain
The music's soft report, and mould the same
In her own murmurs, that whatever mood
His curious fingers lent, her voice made good.
The man perceived his rival and her art;
Disposed to give the light-foot lady sport,
Awakes his lute, and 'gainst the fight to come
Informs it, in a sweet præludium [1]
Of closer strains, and, ere the war begin,
He lightly skirmishes on every string
Charged with a flying touch; and straightway she
Carves out her dainty voice as readily,
Into a thousand sweet distinguish'd tones,
And reckons up in soft divisions

[1] Prelude.

Quick volumes of wild notes, to let him know,
By that shrill taste, she could do something too.
   His nimble hands' instinct then taught each string
A cap'ring cheerfulness, and made them sing
To their own dance ; now negligently rash
He throws his arm, and with a long-drawn dash
Blends all together ; then distinctly trips
From this to that, then quick returning skips
And snatches this again; and pauses there.
She measures every measure, everywhere
Meets art with art ; sometimes, as if in doubt,
Not perfect yet, and fearing to be out,
Trails her plain ditty in one long-spun note,
Through the sleek passage of her open throat,
A clear unwrinkled song ; then doth she point it
With tender accents, and severely joint it
By short diminutives, that being rear'd
In controverting warbles evenly shared,
With her sweet self she wrangles.   He, amazed
That from so small a channel should be raised
The torrent of a voice whose melody
Could melt into such sweet variety,
Strains higher yet, that tickled with rare art
The tattling strings (each breathing in his part),
Most kindly do fall out ; the grumbling base
In surly groans disdains the treble's grace;
The high - perch'd treble chirps at this, and
      chides,
Until his finger (Moderator) hides
And closes the sweet quarrel, rousing all,
Hoarse, shrill, at once, as when the trumpets call
Hot Mars to th' harvest of death's field, and
      woo
Men's hearts into their hands ; this lesson too

She gives him back ; her supple breast thrills out
Sharp airs, and staggers in a warbling doubt
Of dallying sweetness, hovers o'er her skill,
And folds in wav'd notes with a trembling bill
The pliant series of her slippery song ;
Then starts she suddenly into a throng
Of short thick sobs, whose thundering volleys float,
And roll themselves over her lubric [1] throat
In panting murmurs, 'still'd out of her breast,
That ever-bubbling spring, the sugar'd nest
Of her delicious soul, that there does lie
Bathing in streams of liquid melody ;
Music's best seed-plot ; when in ripen'd airs
A golden-headed harvest fairly rears
His honey-dropping tops, plough'd by her breath,
Which there reciprocally laboureth
In that sweet soil ; it seems a holy choir
Founded to th' name of great Apollo's lyre ;
Whose silver-roof rings with the sprightly notes
Of sweet-lipp'd angel-imps, that swill their throats
In cream of morning Helicon, [2] and then
Prefer soft anthems to the ears of men,
To woo them from their beds, still murmuring
That men can sleep while they their matins sing :
(Most divine service) whose so early lay
Prevents [3] the eyelids of the blushing Day.
There might you hear her kindle her soft voice
In the close murmur of a sparkling noise,

[1] Smooth.

[2] A range of mountains snow-capt sacred to Apollo, whence sprung the fountain of the Muses.

[3] Anticipates. Cf. collect for Tuesday in Easter week, Book of Common Prayer : "That as by Thy special grace preventing us."

And lay the ground-work of her hopeful song,
Still keeping in the forward stream, so long,
Till a sweet whirlwind (striving to get out)
Heaves her soft bosom, wanders round about,
And makes a pretty earthquake in her breast,
Till the fledged notes at length forsake their nest,
Fluttering in wanton shoals, and to the sky,
Wing'd with their own wild echoes, prattling
    fly.
She opes the floodgate, and lets loose a tide
Of streaming sweetness, which in state doth ride
On the waved back of every swelling strain,
Rising and falling in a pompous train;
And while she thus discharges a shrill peal
Of flashing airs, she qualifies their zeal
With the cool epode [1] of a graver note,
Thus high, thus low, as if her silver throat
Would reach the brazen voice of War's hoarse
    bird.
Her little soul is ravish'd, and so pour'd
Into loose ecstasies, that she is placed
Above herself, Music's Enthusiast.
   Shame now and anger mixed a double stain
In the Musician's face; "Yet once again
(Mistress) I come; now reach a strain, my lute,
Above her mock, or be for ever mute;
Or tune a song of victory to me,
Or to thyself sing thine own obsequy;"
So said, his hands sprightly as fire he flings,
And with a quavering coyness tastes the strings.
The sweet-lipp'd sisters, musically frighted,
Singing their fears, are fearfully delighted,

---

[1] The stanza following the strophe and antistrophe—
the after song.

Trembling as when Apollo's golden hairs
Are fann'd and frizzled in the wanton airs
Of his own breath, which married to his lyre
Doth tune the spheres, and make Heaven's self
    look higher.
From this to that, from that to this he flies,
Feels Music's pulse in all her arteries ;
Caught in a net which there Apollo spreads,
His fingers struggle with the vocal threads.
Following those little rills, he sinks into
A sea of Helicon ; his hand does go
Those paths of sweetness which with nectar drop,
Softer than that which pants in Hebe's [1] cup.
The humorous strings expound his learnèd touch
By various glosses ; [2] now they seem to grutch,[3]
And murmur in a buzzing din, then gingle
In shrill-tongued accents, striving to be single.
Every smooth turn, every delicious stroke
Gives life to some new grace ; thus doth he invoke
Sweetness by all her names ; thus, bravely thus,
(Fraught with a fury so harmonious)
The Lute's light genius now does proudly rise,
Heaved on the surges of swollen rhapsodies,
Whose flourish (meteor-like) doth curl the air
With flash of high-born fancies ; here and there
Dancing in lofty measures, and anon
Creeps on the soft touch of a tender tone ;
Whose trembling murmurs melting in wild airs
Runs to and fro, complaining [4] his sweet cares,
Because those precious mysteries that dwell
In Music's ravish'd soul he dares not tell,

---

[1] The goddess of youth, who waited on the gods and
filled their cups with nectar.   [2] Sounds.
  [3] Envy, a corruption of grudge.   [4] Bewailing.

But whisper to the world : thus do they vary
Each string his note, as if they meant to carry
Their Master's blest soul (snatch'd out at his
    ears
By a strong ecstasy) through all the spheres
Of Music's heaven ; and seat it there on high
In th' empyrean of pure harmony.
At length (after so long, so loud a strife
Of all the strings, still breathing the best life
Of blest variety, attending on
His fingers' fairest revolution,
In many a sweet rise, many as sweet a fall)
A full-mouth'd diapason swallows all.

    This done, he lists what she would say to this,
And she (although her breath's late exercise
Had dealt too roughly with her tender throat),
Yet summons all her sweet powers for a note.
Alas ! in vain, (for while sweet soul) she tries
To measure all those wild diversities
Of chatt'ring strings, by the small size of one
Poor simple voice, raised in a natural tone ;
She fails, and failing grieves, and grieving dies.
She dies : and leaves her life the Victor's prize,
Falling upon his lute : O, fit to have
(That lived so sweetly) dead, so sweet a grave.

WISHES

TO HIS (SUPPOSED) MISTRESS

WHOE'ER she be,
    That not impossible She,
That shall command my heart and me ;

Where'er she lie,
Lock'd up from mortal eye,
In shady leaves of Destiny :

Till that ripe Birth
Of studied Fate stand forth,
And teach her fair steps tread our Earth ;

Till that divine
Idea take a shrine
Of crystal flesh, through which to shine :

Meet you her, my Wishes,
Bespeak her to my blisses,
And be ye call'd, my absent kisses.

I wish her beauty,
That owes not all its duty
To gaudy tire, or glist'ring shoe-tie,

Something more than
Taffeta [1] or tissue [2] can,
Or rampant feather, or rich fan,

More than the spoil
Of shop, or silkworm's toil,
Or a bought blush, or a set smile ;

A face that's best
By its own beauty dress'd,
And can alone commend the rest,—

A face made up
Out of no other shop
Than what Nature's white hand sets ope ;

[1] A thin silk.
[2] A cloth interwoven with gold or silver or figured colours.

A cheek where youth
And blood, with pen of Truth,
Write what their reader sweetly ru'th,—[1]

A cheek where grows
More than a morning rose,
Which to no box its being owes;

Lips, where all day
A lover's kiss may play,
Yet carry nothing thence away;

Looks that oppress
Their richest tires,[2] but dress
Themselves in simple nakedness;

Eyes, that displace
The neighbour diamond, and out-face
That sunshine by their own sweet grace;

Tresses, that wear
Jewels, but to declare
How much themselves more precious are,—

Whose native ray
Can tame the wanton day
Of gems that in their bright shades play,—

Each ruby there
Or pearl that dare appear,
Be its own blush, be its own tear.

A well-tamed Heart,
For whose more noble smart
Love may be long choosing a dart.

[1] Rueth—laments.   [2] Attire.

Eyes that bestow
Full quivers on Love's bow,
Yet pay less arrows than they owe.

Smiles that can warm
The blood, yet teach a charm
That chastity shall take no harm.

Blushes that bin [1]
The burnish of no sin,
Nor flames of aught too hot within.

Joys that confess
Virtue their Mistress,
And have no other head to dress.

Fears fond, and flight,[2]
As the coy bride's when night
First does the longing lover right.

Tears quickly fled
And vain, as those are shed
For a dying maidenhead.

Days that need borrow
No part of their good morrow
From a fore-spent night of sorrow,—

Days that, in spite
Of darkness, by the light
Of a clear mind are day all night;

Nights sweet as they,
Made short by lovers' play,
Yet long by the absence of the day.

[1] Blushes that *are*. Bin being an old form of be—been.
[2] Fleeting.

Life that dares send
A challenge to his end,
And when it comes say, Welcome, friend !

Sidneian [1] showers
Of sweet discourse, whose powers
Can crown old Winter's head with flowers ;

Soft silken hours,
Open suns, shady bowers ;
'Bove all, nothing within that lours ; [2]

Whate'er delight
Can make Day's forehead bright
Or give down to the wings of Night.

In her whole frame
Have Nature all the name,
Art and Ornament the shame.

Her flattery
Picture and Poesy,
Her counsel her own virtue be.

I wish her store
Of worth may leave her poor
Of wishes ; and I wish—no more.

Now if Time knows
That Her, whose radiant brows
Weave them a garland of my vows—

[1] Refers to Sir Philip Sidney, author of *Arcadia*, a very popular book in Crashaw's day, famous among other things for its euphuism.
[2] Is threatening.

Her whose just bays
My future hopes can raise
A trophy to her present praise,

Her that dares be
What these lines wish to see—
I seek no further—it is She.

'Tis She, and here
Lo! I unclothe and clear
My Wishes' cloudy character.

May She enjoy it
Whose merit dares apply it,
But Modesty dares still deny it.

Such Worth as this is
Shall fix my flying wishes,
And determine them to kisses.

Let her full glory,
My fancies, fly before ye!
Be you my fictions, but her story.

WITH A PICTURE SENT TO A FRIEND

I PAINT so ill, my piece had need to be
    Painted again by some good poesy.
I write so ill, my slender line is scarce
So much as th' picture of a well-limn'd verse:
Yet may the love I send be true, though I
Send nor true picture nor true poesy:
Both which away, I should not need to fear
My love, or feign'd, or painted should appear.

UPON BISHOP ANDREWES'S
PICTURE BEFORE HIS SERMONS

THIS reverend shadow cast that setting sun,
  Whose glorious course through our horizon
    run,
Left the dim face of this dull hemisphere
All one great eye, all drown'd in one great tear;
Whose fair illustrious soul led his free thought
Through Learning's universe, and (vainly) sought
Room for her spacious self, until at length
She found the way home with an holy strength,
Snatch'd herself hence to Heaven; fill'd a bright
    place
'Mongst those immortal fires, and on the face
Of her great Maker fixed her flaming eye,
There still to read true, pure divinity.
And now that grave aspect hath deign'd to shrink
Into this less appearance.   If you think
'Tis but a dead face Art doth here bequeath,
Look on the following leaves, and see him breathe.

UPON THE DEATH OF A
GENTLEMAN

FAITHLESS and fond Mortality,
  Who will ever credit thee?
Fond and faithless thing, that thus
In our best hopes beguilest us.
What a reckoning hast thou made
Of the hopes in him we laid!

For life by volumes lengthenèd,
A line or two to speak him dead.
For the laurel in his verse
The sullen cypress o'er his hearse ;
For so many hopèd years
Of fruit, so many fruitless tears ;
For a silver-crownèd head
A dirty pillow in Death's bed.
For so dear, so deep a trust,
Sad requital, thus much dust.
Now though the blow that snatcht him hence
Stopp'd the mouth of Eloquence,
Though she be dumb e'er since his death,
Not used to speak but in his breath,
Leaving his death ungarnishèd
Therefore ; because he is dead.
Yet if at least she not denies
The sad language of our eyes,
We are contented : for than this
Language none more fluent is.
Nothing speaks our grief so well
As to speak nothing.   Come then, tell
Thy mind in tears, whoe'er thou be
That ow'st a name to misery :
Eyes are vocal, tears have tongues,
And there be words not made with lungs,
Sententious showers, O, let them fall,
Their cadence is rhetorical.
Here's a theme will drink th' expense
Of all thy watery eloquence ;
Weep then, only be exprest
Thus much : He's dead ; and weep the rest

UPON THE DEATH OF MR. HERRYS

A PLANT of noble stem, forward and fair,
　As ever whisper'd to the morning air,
Thrived in these happy grounds, the Earth's just
　　pride,
Whose rising glories made such haste to hide
His head in clouds, as if in him alone
Impatient Nature had taught motion
To start from Time, and cheerfully to fly
Before, and seize upon Maturity.
Thus grew this gracious plant, in whose sweet
　　shade
The sun himself oft wish'd to sit, and made
The morning Muses perch like birds, and sing
Among his branches : yea, and vow'd to bring
His own delicious phœnix from the blest
Arabia, there to build her virgin nest,
To hatch herself in ; 'mongst his leaves, the Day
Fresh from the rosy East, rejoiced to play ;
To them she gave the first and fairest beam
That waited on her birth : she gave to them
The purest pearls, that wept her evening death ;
The balmy Zephyrus got so sweet a breath
By often kissing them ; and now begun
Glad Time to ripen Expectation.
The timorous maiden-blossoms on each bough
Peeped forth from their first blushes ; so that now
A thousand ruddy hopes smiled in each bud,
And flatter'd every greedy eye that stood
Fixed in delight, as if already there
Those rare fruits dangled, whence the golden Year

His crown expected, when (O Fate ! O Time !
That seldom let'st a blushing youthful prime
Hide his hot beams in shade of silver Age,
So rare is hoary Virtue) the dire rage
Of a mad storm these bloomy joys all tore,
Ravish'd the maiden blossoms, and down bore
The trunk.   Yet in this ground his precious root
Still lives, which when weak Time shall be poured
     out
Into Eternity, and circular [1] joys
Dance in an endless round, again shall rise
The fair son of an ever-youthful Spring,
To be a shade for angels while they sing.
Meanwhile, whoe'er thou art that passest here,
O do thou water it with one kind tear.

UPON THE DEATH OF THE MOST
DESIRED MR. HERRYS

DEATH, what dost ? O, hold thy blow,
        What thou dost thou dost not know
Death, thou must not here be cruel,
This is Nature's choicest jewel :
This is he, in whose rare frame
Nature labour'd for a name :
And meant to leave his precious feature
The pattern of a perfect creature.
Joy of Goodness, Love of Art,
Virtue wears him next her heart.
Him the Muses love to follow,
Him they call their vice-Apollo.

[1] Unending.

Apollo, golden though thou be,
Th' art not fairer than is he,
Nor more lovely lift'st thy head,
(Blushing) from thine Eastern bed.
The glories of thy youth ne'er knew
Brighter hopes than he can show,
Why then should it e'er be seen
That his should fade, while thine is
    green?
And wilt thou (O, cruel boast!)
Put poor Nature to such cost?
O, 'twill undo our common mother,
To be at charge of such another.
What! think we to no other end
Gracious heavens do use to send
Earth her best perfection,
But to vanish, and be gone?
Therefore only given to-day,
To-morrow to be snatch'd away?
   I've seen indeed the hopeful bud
Of a ruddy rose that stood
Blushing, to behold the ray
Of the new-saluted Day:
(His tender top not fully spread)
The sweet dash of a shower new-shed
Invited him no more to hide
Within himself the purple pride
Of his forward flower, when lo
While he sweetly 'gan to show
His swelling glories, Auster [1] spied him,
Cruel Auster thither hied him,
And with the rush of one rude blast,
Shamed not spitefully to waste

      [1] The Sirocco of Italy.

All his leaves, so fresh, so sweet,
And lay them trembling at his feet.
   I've seen the Morning's lovely ray
Hover o'er the new-born Day
With rosy wings so richly bright
As if he scorned to think of Night;
When a rugged storm whose scowl
Made heaven's radiant face look foul,
Called for an untimely night
To blot the newly-blossomed light.
But were the rose's blush so rare,
Were the Morning's smile so fair,
As is he, nor cloud, nor wind
But would be courteous, would be kind.
   Spare him, Death! ah! spare him then,
Spare the sweetest among men!
And let not Pity, with her tears,
Keep such distance from thine ears;
But O, thou wilt not, canst not spare,
Haste hath never time to hear.
Therefore if he needs must go,
And the Fates will have it so,
Softly may he be possessed
Of his monumental rest.
Safe, thou dark home of the dead,
Safe, O hide his lovèd head.
Keep him close, close in thine arms
Sealed up with a thousand charms.
For Pity's sake, O, hide him quite
From his mother Nature's sight;
Lest, for grief his loss may move,
All her births abortive prove.

ANOTHER

IF ever Pity were acquainted
   With stern Death, if e'er he fainted,
Or forgot the cruel vigour,
Of an adamantine rigour,
Here, O here we should have known it,
Here, or nowhere, he'd have shown it.
For he whose precious memory
Bathes in tears of every eye :
He to whom our sorrow brings
All the streams of all her springs,
Was so rich in grace and nature,
In all the gifts that bless a creature,
The fresh hopes of his lovely youth
Flourish'd in so fair a growth ;
So sweet the temple was, that shrined
The sacred sweetness of his mind ;
That could the Fates know to relent,
Could they know what mercy meant,
Or had ever learn'd to bear
The soft tincture of a tear,
Tears would now have flowed so deep,
As might have taught Grief how to weep.
Now all their steely operation,
Would quite have lost the cruel fashion.
Sickness would have gladly been
Sick himself to have saved him ;
And his fever wished to prove
Burning only in his love.
Him when Wrath itself had seen,
Wrath itself had lost his spleen.

Grim Destruction here amazed,
Instead of striking, would have gazed.
Even the iron-pointed pen,
That notes the tragic dooms of men,
Wet with tears 'still'd from the eyes
Of the flinty Destinies,
Would have learned a softer style,
And have been ashamed to spoil
His life's sweet story, by the haste
Of a cruel stop ill-placed.
In the dark volume of our fate,
Whence each leaf of life hath date,
Where in sad particulars
The total sum of man appears ;
And the short clause of mortal breath,
Bound in the period of Death :
In all the book, if anywhere
Such a term as this, Spare here,
Could have been found, 'twould have been read,
Writ in white letters o'er his head :
Or close unto his name annexed,
The fair gloss of a fairer text.
In brief, if any one were free,
He was that one, and only he.

But he, alas ! even he is dead,
And our hopes' fair harvest spread
In the dust.   Pity, now spend
All the tears that Grief can lend.
Sad Mortality may hide
In his ashes all her pride ;
With this inscription o'er his head :
" All hope of never dying, here is dead."

HIS EPITAPH

PASSENGER, whoe'er thou art,
    Stay awhile, and let thy heart
Take acquaintance of this stone,
Before thou passest further on ;
This stone will tell thee, that beneath
Is entombed the crime of Death ;
The ripe endowments of whose mind
Left his years so much behind,
That numbering of his virtues' praise,
Death lost the reckoning of his days ;
And believing what they told,
Imagined him exceeding old.
In him Perfection did set forth
The strength of her united worth ;
Him his wisdom's pregnant [1] growth
Made so reverend, even in youth,
That in the centre of his breast
(Sweet as is the phœnix' nest)
Every reconcilèd grace
Had their general meeting-place.
In him Goodness joy'd to see
Learning learn humility ;
The splendour of his birth and blood
Was but the gloss of his own good.
The flourish of his sober youth
Was the pride of naked truth.
In composure of his face
Lived a fair, but manly grace ;
His mouth was Rhetoric's best mould,
His tongue the touchstone of her gold.

[1] Fruitful.

What word soe'er his breath kept warm,
Was no word now but a charm;
For all persuasive Graces thence
Sucked their sweetest influence.
His virtue that within had root,
Could not choose but shine without;
And th' heart-bred lustre of his worth,
At each corner peeping forth,
Pointed him out in all his ways,
Circled round in his own rays:
That to his sweetness all men's eyes
Were vow'd Love's flaming sacrifice.

Him while fresh and fragrant Time
Cherish'd in his golden prime;
Ere Hebe's hand had overlaid
His smooth cheeks with a downy shade;
The rush of Death's unruly wave
Swept him off into his grave.

Enough, now (if thou canst) pass on,
For now (alas!) not in this stone
(Passenger, whoe'er thou art)
Is he entomb'd, but in thy heart.

AN EPITAPH UPON MR. ASHTON, A COMFORTABLE CITIZEN

THE modest front of this small floor,
    Believe me, Reader, can say more
Than many a braver marble can,
"Here lies a truly honest man."
One whose conscience was a thing
That troubled neither Church nor King.

One of those few that in this town
Honour all Preachers, hear their own.
Sermons he heard, yet not so many
As left no time to practise any.
He heard them reverently, and then
His practice preached them o'er again.
His Parlour-Sermons rather were
Those to the eye than to the ear.
His prayers took their price and strength
Not from the loudness, nor the length.
He was a Protestant at home
Not only in despite of Rome.
He loved his Father; yet his zeal
Tore not off his Mother's [1] veil.
To th' Church he did allow her dress,[2]
True Beauty, to true Holiness.
Peace, which he loved in life, did lend
Her hand to bring him to his end.
When Age and Death called for the score
No surfeits were to reckon for.
Death tore not—therefore—but sans [3] strife
Gently untwined his thread of life.
What remains then but that thou
Write these lines, Reader, in thy brow,
And by his fair example's light
Burn in thy imitation bright.
So while these lines can but bequeath
A life perhaps unto his death;
His better Epitaph shall be
His life still kept alive in thee.

[1] The Holy Catholic Church established in England.
[2] A reference to the vestments of the priest, interesting
to us at the present time. Cf. Ornaments Rubric.
[3] Without.

AN EPITAPH ON A YOUNG MARRIED COUPLE DEAD AND BURIED TOGETHER

TO these, whom Death again did wed,
   This grave's their second marriage-bed ;
For though the hand of Fate could force
'Twixt soul and body, a divorce,
It could not sunder man and wife,
'Cause they both livèd but one life.
Peace, good Reader, do not weep.
Peace, the lovers are asleep.
They, sweet turtles, folded lie
In the last knot that Love could tie.
And though they lie as they were dead,
Their pillow stone, their sheets of lead :
Pillow hard, and sheets not warm,
Love made the bed ; they'll take no harm ;
Let them sleep : let them sleep on,
Till this stormy night be gone,
And the eternal morrow dawn ;
Then the curtains will be drawn
And they wake into a light,
Whose Day shall never sleep in Night.

DEATH'S LECTURE AND THE FUNERAL OF A YOUNG GENTLEMAN

DEAR relics of a dislodged soul, whose lack
   Makes many a mourning paper put on black !
O stay a while, ere thou draw in thy head,
And wind thyself up close in thy cold bed.

Stay but a little while, until I call
A summons worthy of thy funeral.
Come then, Youth, Beauty, (and) Blood, all ye
    soft powers,
Whose silken flatteries swell a few fond hours
Into a false eternity.   Come man ;
Hyperbolisèd nothing ! know thy span.
Take thine own measure here, down, down, and
    bow
Before thyself in thine idea ; thou
Huge emptiness ! contract thy bulk ; and shrink
All thy wide circle to a point.   O sink
Lower and lower yet ; till thy lean size,
Call Heaven to look on thee with narrow eyes.
Lesser and lesser yet ; till thou begin
To show a face, fit to confess thy kin,
Thy neighbourhood to Nothing !
Proud looks, and lofty eyelids, here put on
Yourselves in your unfeign'd reflection ;
Here, gallant ladies ! [1] this unpartial glass
(Through all your painting) shows you your true
    face.
These death-seal'd lips are they dare give the lie
To the loud boasts of poor Mortality ;
These curtain'd windows, this self-prison'd eye
Out-stares the lids of large-look'd Tyranny :
This posture is the brave one ; this that lies
Thus low, stands up (methinks) thus, and defies
The World.   All - daring dust and ashes ! only
    you
Of all interpreters read Nature true.

  [1] This is very reminiscent of the celebrated fresco " The
Triumph of Death " in the Campo Santo at Pisa.

AN EPITAPH UPON DOCTOR BROOK

A BROOK, whose stream so great, so good,
     Was loved, was honour'd as a flood.
Whose banks the Muses dwelt upon,
More than their own Helicon,
Here at length hath gladly found
A quiet passage under ground;
Meanwhile his lovèd banks, now dry,
The Muses with their tears supply.

ON A FOUL MORNING, BEING THEN
TO TAKE A JOURNEY

WHERE art thou, Sol, while thus the blind-
          fold Day
Staggers out of the East, loses her way,
Stumbling on Night? Rouse thee, illustrious
     youth,
And let no dull mists choke thy Light's fair growth.
Point here thy beams; O, glance on yonder flocks,
And make their fleeces golden as thy locks!
Unfold thy fair front, and there shall appear
Full glory flaming in her own free sphere.
Gladness shall clothe the Earth, we will instile
The face of things an universal smile:
Say to the sullen Morn thou com'st to court her,
And wilt demand proud Zephyrus to sport her
With wanton gales; his balmy breath shall lick
The tender drops which tremble on her cheek;

Which rarefied, and in a gentle rain
On those delicious banks distill'd again,
Shall rise in a sweet Harvest, which discloses
Two ever-blushing beds of new-born roses.
He'll fan her bright locks, teaching them to flow,
And frisk in curl'd meanders: [1] he will throw
A fragrant breath suck'd from the spicy nest
O' th' precious phœnix, warm upon her breast.
He with a dainty and soft hand will trim
And brush her azure mantle, which shall swim
In silken volumes; wheresoe'er she'll tread
Bright clouds like golden fleeces shall be spread.
　Rise then (fair blue-eyed maid!) rise and dis-
　　cover
Thy silver brow, and meet thy golden lover.
See how he runs, with what a hasty flight,
Into thy bosom, bath'd with liquid light.
Fly, fly profane fogs, far hence fly away,
Taint not the pure streams of the springing Day,
With your dull influence; it is for you
To sit and scowl upon Night's heavy brow,
Not on the fresh cheeks of the virgin Morn,
Where naught but smiles and ruddy joys are worn.
Fly then, and do not think with her to stay;
Let it suffice, she'll wear no mask to-day.

TO THE MORNING

SATISFACTION FOR SLEEP

WHAT succour can I hope the Muse will
　　send
Whose drowsiness hath wrong'd the Muses' friend?

[1] Serpentine windings.

What hope, Aurora, to propitiate thee,
Unless the Muse sing my apology?
O in that morning of my shame, when I
Lay folded up in sleep's captivity,
How at the sight didst thou draw back thine
    eyes
Into thy modest veil, how didst thou rise
Twice dyed in thine own blushes, and didst
    run
To draw the curtains, and awake the sun;
Who, rousing his illustrious tresses, came,
And seeing the loath'd object, hid for shame
His head in thy fair bosom, and still hides
Me from his patronage; I pray, he chides.
And pointing to dull Morpheus, bids me take
My own Apollo, try if I can make
His Lethe [1] be my Helicon: and see
If Morpheus [2] have a Muse to wait on me.
Hence 'tis, my humble fancy finds no wings,
No nimble rapture starts to Heaven, and brings
Enthusiastic flames, such as can give
Marrow to my plump genius, make it live
Drest in the glorious madness of a Muse,
Whose feet can walk the Milky-way, and choose
Her starry throne; whose holy heats can warm
The grave, and hold up an exalted arm
To lift me from my lazy urn, to climb
Upon the stooping shoulders of old Time,
And trace Eternity.—But all is dead,
All these delicious hopes are burièd
In the deep wrinkles of his angry brow,
Where Mercy cannot find them: but O thou

[1] The river of oblivion.
[2] The son of sleep and the god of dreams.

Bright lady of the Morn! pity doth lie
So warm in thy soft breast, it cannot die.
Have mercy then, and when he next shall rise,
O meet the angry God, invade his eyes,
And stroke his radiant cheeks; one timely kiss
Will kill his anger, and revive my bliss.
So to the treasure of thy pearly dew
Thrice will I pay these tears, to show how true
My grief is; so my wakeful lay shall knock
At th' oriental gates, and duly mock
The early larks' shrill orizons,[1] to be
An anthem at the Day's nativity.
And the same rosy-finger'd hand of thine,
That shuts Night's dying eyes, shall open mine.

   But thou, faint God of Sleep, forget that I
Was ever known to be thy votary.
No more my pillow shall thine altar be,
Nor will I offer any more to thee
Myself a melting sacrifice; I'm born
Again a fresh child of the buxom Morn,
Heir of the sun's first beams; why threat'st thou so?
Why dost thou shake thy leaden sceptre? Go,
Bestow thy poppy upon wakeful Woe,
Sickness, and Sorrow, whose pale lids ne'er know
Thy downy finger; dwell upon their eyes,
Shut in their tears: shut out their miseries.

LOVE'S HOROSCOPE

LOVE, brave Virtue's younger Brother,
   Erst hath made my heart a mother;
She consults the conscious Spheres
To calculate her young son's years.

[1] Prayers.

She asks if sad or saving powers
Gave omen to his infant hours;
She asks each star that then stood by
If poor Love shall live or die.

Ah! my heart, is that the way?
Are these the beams that rule thy day?
Thou know'st a face, in whose each look,
Beauty lays ope Love's fortune-book,
On whose fair revolutions wait
The obsequious motions of Love's fate;
Ah! my heart, her eyes and she
Have taught thee new astrology.
Howe'er Love's native hours were set,
Whatever starry synod met,
'Tis in the mercy of her eye,
If poor Love shall live or die.

If those sharp rays, putting on
Points of death, bid Love be gone,
(Though the Heavens in counsel sate,
To crown an uncontrollèd fate,
Though their best aspects twined upon
The kindest constellation,
Cast amorous glances on his birth,
And whisper'd the confed'rate Earth
To pave his paths with all the good
That warms the bed of youth and blood,)
Love has no plea against her eye:
Beauty frowns, and Love must die.

But if her milder influence move,
And gild the hopes of humble Love:
(Though Heaven's inauspicious eye
Lay black on Love's nativity;

Though every diamond in Jove's crown
Fixed his forehead to a frown,)
Her eye a strong appeal can give,
Beauty smiles, and Love shall live.

O if Love shall live, O, where
But in her eye, or in her ear,
In her breast, or in her breath,
Shall I hide poor Love from Death?
For in the life aught else can give,
Love shall die, although he live.

Or if Love shall die, O, where,
But in her eye, or in her ear,
In her breath, or in her breast,
Shall I build his funeral nest?
While Love shall thus entombed lie,
Love shall live, although he die.

UPON THE FRONTISPIECE OF MR. ISAACSON'S CHRONOLOGY

LET hoary Time's vast bowels be the grave
    To what his bowels' birth and being gave;
Let Nature die, and (Phœnix-like) from death
Revivèd Nature take a second breath;
If on Time's right hand sit fair History,
If, from the seed of empty Ruin, she
Can raise so fair an harvest, let her be
Ne'er so far distant, yet Chronology
(Sharp-sighted as the eagle's eye, that can
Out-stare the broad-beam'd Day's meridian)
Will have a perspicil [1] to find her out,
And, through the night of error and dark doubt,

[1] An optic glass.

Discern the dawn of Truth's eternal ray,
As when the rosy Morn buds into day.
  Now that Time's empire might be amply fill'd,
Babel's bold artists strive (below) to build
Ruin a temple, on whose fruitful fall
History rears her pyramids, more tall
Than were th' Egyptian (by the life these give
Th' Egyptian pyramids themselves must live);
On these she lifts the world, and on their base
Shows the two terms and limits of Time's race:
That the Creation is; the Judgment this;
That the World's morning; this, her midnight is.

TO THE QUEEN[1]

AN APOLOGY FOR THE LENGTH OF THE FOLLOWING PANEGYRIC

WHEN you are mistress of the song,
    Mighty queen, to think it long,
Were treason 'gainst that majesty
Your Virtue wears. Your modesty
Yet thinks it so. But even that too
(Infinite, since part of you)
New matter for our Muse supplies,
And so allows what it denies.
Say then, dread Queen, how may we do
To mediate 'twixt yourself and you?
That so our sweetly-temper'd song
Nor be too short, nor seem too long,
    Needs must your noble praises' strength,
    That made it long, excuse the length.
      [1] Henrietta Maria.

TO THE QUEEN

UPON HER NUMEROUS PROGENY : A PANEGYRIC

BRITAIN, the mighty Ocean's lovely bride,
  Now stretch thyself (fair Isle) and grow;
    spread wide
Thy bosom, and make room.   Thou art opprest
With thine own glories : and art strangely blest
Beyond thyself: for, lo ! the gods, the gods
Come fast upon thee ; and those glorious odds
Swell thy full glories to a pitch so high
As sits above thy best capacity.
  Are they not odds ? and glorious ? that to thee
Those mighty genii throng, which well might be
Each one an age's labour, that thy days
Are gilded with the union of those rays
Whose each divided beam would be a sun,
To glad the sphere of any nation ?
Sure if for these thou mean'st to find a seat,
Thou hast need, O Britain, to be truly Great.
  And so thou art; their presence makes thee
    so :
They are thy greatness.   Gods, where'er they go,
Bring their Heaven with them ; their great foot-
    steps place
An everlasting smile upon the face
Of the glad Earth they tread on ; while with thee
Those beams that ampliate mortality,
And teach it to expatiate, and swell
To majesty and fulness, deign to dwell ;
Thou by thyself may'st sit (blest Isle), and see
How thy great mother Nature dotes on thee :

Thee therefore from the rest apart she hurl'd,
And seem'd to make an Isle, but made a world.
Time yet hath dropt few plumes since Hope turned
    Joy,
And took into his arms the princely Boy,
Whose birth last blest the bed of his sweet mother,
And bade us first salute our prince, a brother.

The Prince and Duke of York

BRIGHT Charles! thou sweet dawn of a glorious
    day,
Centre of those thy grandsires (shall I say
Henry and James? or Mars and Phœbus rather?
If this were Wisdom's god, that War's stern father,
'Tis but the same is said, Henry and James
Are Mars and Phœbus under divers names).
O thou full mixture of those mighty souls.
Whose vast intelligences tuned the poles
Of peace and war; thou for whose manly brow
Both laurels twine into one wreath, and woo
To be thy garland; see (sweet Prince), O see,
Thou, and the lovely hopes that smile in thee,
Are ta'en out, and transcribed by thy great
    Mother.
See, see thy real shadow; see thy brother,
Thy little self in less: trace in these eyne
The beams that dance in those full stars of thine.
From the same snowy alabaster rock
Those hands and thine were hewn; those cherries
    mock
The coral of thy lips. Thou wert of all
This well-wrought copy the fair principal.

Lady Mary

JUSTLY, great Nature, didst thou brag and tell
How even th' hadst drawn that faithful parallel,
And matched thy master-piece. O then, go on,
Make such another sweet comparison.
See'st thou that Mary there? O, teach her
   mother
To show her to herself in such another:
Fellow [1] this wonder too, nor let her shine
Alone; light such another star, and twine
Their rosy beams, so that the morn for one
Venus, may have a constellation.

Lady Elizabeth

THESE words scarce wakened Heaven, when, lo!
   our vows
Sat crowned upon the noble infant's brows.
Thou'st paired, sweet princess: in this well-writ
   book
Read o'er thyself; peruse each line, each look.
And when th' hast summed up all those blooming
   blisses,
Close up the book, and clasp it with thy kisses.
So have I seen (to dress their mistress May)
Two silken sister-flowers consult, and lay
Their bashful cheeks together; newly they
Peeped from their buds, showed like the garden's
   eyes
Scarce waked: like was the crimson of their joys,
Like were the tears they wept, so like, that one
Seemed but the other's kind reflection.

             [1] Match.

The New-born Prince

AND now 'twere time to say, sweet Queen, no
      more.
Fair source of Princes, is thy precious store
Not yet exhaust? O no! Heavens have no bound,
But in their infinite and endless round
Embrace themselves. Our measure is not theirs;
Nor may the poverty of man's narrow prayers
Span their immensity. More princes come:
Rebellion, stand thou by; Mischief, make room:
War, Blood, and Death (names all averse from
      Joy)
Hear this, we have another bright-eyed boy:
That word's a warrant, by whose virtue I
Have full authority to bid you die.
      Die, die, foul misbegotten monsters! die,
Make haste away, or e'er the World's bright eye
Blush to a cloud of blood. O far from men
Fly hence, and in your Hyperborean [1] den
Hide you for evermore, and murmur there
Where none but Hell may hear, nor our soft air
Shrink at the hateful sound. Meanwhile we bear,
High as the brow of Heaven, the noble noise
And name of these our just and righteous joys,
Where Envy shall not reach them, nor those Ears
Whose tune keeps time to aught below the spheres.
      But thou, sweet supernumerary star,
Shine forth; nor fear the threats of boisterous
      War.
The face of things has therefore frowned a while
On purpose that to thee and thy pure smile

      [1] Northern.

13

The World might owe an universal calm;
While thou, fair halcyon,[1] on a sea of balm
Shalt float; where, while thou lay'st thy lovely head,
The angry billows shall but make thy bed:
Storms, when they look on thee, shall straight
 relent;
And tempests, when they taste thy breath, repent
To whispers, soft as thine own slumbers be,
Or souls of virgins which shall sigh for thee.
 Shine then, sweet supernumerary star,
Nor fear the boisterous names of blood and war:
Thy birthday is their death's nativity;
They've here no other business but to die.

To the Queen

But stay; what glimpse was that? why blushed the
 Day?
Why ran the startled air trembling away?
Who's this that comes circled in rays that scorn
Acquaintance with the Sun? what second morn
At midday opes a presence which Heaven's eye
Stands off and points at?   Is't some deity
Stept from her throne of stars, deigns to be seen?
Is it some deity? or is't our queen?
 'Tis she, 'tis she: her awful beauties chase
The Day's abashèd glories, and in face
Of noon wear their own sunshine.   O thou bright
Mistress of wonders, Cynthia's is the Night;
But thou at noon dost shine, and art all day
(Nor does thy sun deny it) our Cynthia.
 Illustrious sweetness! in thy faithful womb,
That nest of heroes, all our hopes find room.

---

[1] A bird that comes with calm weather.

Thou art the mother-phœnix, and thy breast
Chaste as that virgin honour of the East,
But much more fruitful is ; nor does, as she,
Deny to mighty Love, a deity.
Then let the Eastern world brag and be proud
Of one coy phœnix, while we have a brood,
A brood of phœnixes : while we have brother
And sister-phœnixes, and still the mother.
    And may we long—Long may'st thou live t'
      increase
The house and family of phœnixes.
Nor may the life that gives their eyelids light
E'er prove the dismal morning of thy night :
Ne'er may a birth of thine be bought so dear
To make his costly cradle of thy bier.
    O may'st thou thus make all the year thine own,
And see such names of joy sit white upon
The brow of every month ; and when thou hast
      done,
May'st in a son of his find every son
Repeated, and that son still in another,
And so in each child, often prove a mother.
Long may'st thou, laden with such clusters, lean
Upon thy royal elm (fair vine,) and when
The heavens will stay no longer, may thy glory
And name dwell sweet in some eternal story.
    Pardon, bright Excellence, an untuned string,
That in thy ears thus keeps a murmuring.
O speak a lowly Muse's pardon, speak
Her pardon, or her sentence ; only break
Thy silence. Speak, and she shall take from thence
Numbers and sweetness, and an influence
Confessing thee.   Or (if too long I stay)
O speak thou, and my pipe hath nought to say :

For see Apollo all this while stands mute,
Expecting by thy voice to tune his lute.
   But gods are gracious ; and their altars make
Precious the offerings that their altars take.
Give them this rural wreath fire from thine eyes ;
This rural wreath dares be thy sacrifice.

UPON TWO GREEN APRICOTS SENT
TO COWLEY BY MR. CRASHAW

TAKE these, Time's tardy truants, sent by me
    To be chastised (sweet friend) and chid by
      thee.
Pale sons of our Pomona ! whose wan cheeks
Have spent the patience of expecting weeks,
Yet are scarce ripe enough at best to show
The red, but of the blush to thee they owe.
By thy comparison they shall put on
More summer in their shame's reflection,
Than e'er the fruitful Phœbus' flaming kisses
Kindled on their cold lips. O had my wishes,
And the dear merits of your Muse, their due,
The year had found some fruit early as you ;
Ripe as those rich composures Time computes
Blossoms, but our blest taste confesses fruits.
How does thy April-Autumn mock these cold
Progressions 'twixt whose terms poor Time grows
    old !
With thee alone he wears no beard, thy brain
Gives him the morning world's fresh gold again.
'Twas only Paradise, 'tis only thou,
Whose fruit and blossoms both bless the same bough,

Proud in the pattern of thy precious youth,
Nature (methinks) might easily mend her growth.
Could she in all her births but copy thee,
Into the public years' proficiency,
No fruit should have the face to smile on thee
(Young master of the World's maturity)
But such whose sun-born beauties what they borrow
Of beams to-day, pay back again to-morrow,
Nor need be double-gilt.   How then must these
Poor fruits look pale at thy Hesperides!
Fain would I chide their slowness, but in their
Defects I draw mine own dull character.
Take them, and me in them acknowledging
How much my Summer waits upon thy Spring.

ALEXIAS[1]

THE COMPLAINT OF THE FORSAKEN WIFE OF SAINT ALEXIS

The First Elegy

I, LATE the Roman youths' loud praise and
       pride,
Whom long none could obtain, though thousands
    tried;
Lo, here am left (alas!) for my lost mate
T' embrace my tears and kiss an unkind fate.
Sure in my early woes stars were at strife,
And tried to make a widow ere a wife.
Nor can I tell (and this new tears doth breed)
In what strange path my lord's fair footsteps bleed.

[1] From the Latin.

O knew I where he wander'd I should see
Some solace in my sorrow's certainty:
I'd send my woes in words should weep for me.
(Who knows how powerful well - writ prayers
    would be?)
Sending's too slow a word; myself would fly.
Who knows my own heart's woes so well as I?
But how shall I steal hence?   Alexis,[1] thou,
Ah, thou thyself, alas! hast taught me how.
Love too, that leads the way, would lend the wings
To bear me harmless through the hardest things.
And where Love lends the wing, and leads the way,
What dangers can there be dare say me nay?
If I be shipwrecked, Love shall teach to swim;
If drown'd, sweet is the death endured for him;
The noted sea shall change his name with me,
I 'mongst the blest stars a new name shall be;
And sure where lovers make their wat'ry graves,
The weeping mariner will augment the waves.
For who so hard, but passing by that way
Will take acquaintance of my woes, and say,
"Here 't was the Roman maid found a hard fate,
While through the World she sought her wand'ring
    mate;
Here perish'd she, poor heart; Heavens, be my
    vows
As true to me as she was to her spouse.

[1] St. Alexis or Alexius, born in Rome in the fifth century, was the son of a rich senator in Rome. Having married a noble Roman lady he deserted her on the day of their marriage, retired to a far country, living in poverty in a house dedicated to the B.V.M. After a time he returned to Rome, and unrecognised lived in his father's house as a poor servant. A little before he died he discovered himself to his parents.

O live, so rare a love! live! and in thee
The too frail life of female constancy.
Farewell; and shine, fair soul, shine there above,
Firm in thy crown, as here fast in thy love.
There thy lost fugitive thou hast found at last:
Be happy; and for ever hold him fast."

The Second Elegy

THOUGH all the joys I had fled hence with thee,
Unkind! yet are my tears still true to me:
I'm wedded o'er again since thou art gone,
Nor couldst thou, cruel, leave me quite alone.
Alexis' widow now is Sorrow's wife;
With him shall I weep out my weary life.
Welcome, my sad-sweet mate! Now have I got
At last a constant Love, that leaves me not:
Firm he, as thou art false; nor need my cries
Thus vex the Earth and tear the beauteous skies.
For him, alas, ne'er shall I need to be
Troublesome to the world, thus, as for thee:
For thee I talk to trees; with silent groves
Expostulate my woes and much wrong'd loves;
Hills and relentless rocks, or if there be
Things that in hardness more allude to thee,
To these I talk in tears, and tell my pain,
And answer too for them in tears again.
How oft have I wept out the weary sun;
My wat'ry hour-glass hath old Time outrun.
O I am learnèd grown: poor Love and I
Have studied over all Astrology;
I'm perfect in Heaven's state, with every star
My skilful grief is grown familiar.

Rise, fairest of those fires; whate'er thou be
Whose rosy beam shall point my sun to me,
Such as the sacred light that erst did bring
The Eastern princes to their infant King.
O rise, pure lamp, and lend thy golden ray,
That weary Love at last may find his way.

The Third Elegy

RICH, churlish Land, that hid'st so long in thee
My treasures; rich, alas, by robbing me.
Needs must my miseries owe that man a spite,
Whoe'er he be, was the first wand'ring knight.
O had he ne'er been at that cruel cost
Nature's virginity had ne'er been lost;
Seas had not been rebuked by saucy oars,
But lain lock'd up safe in their sacred shores;
Men had not spurn'd at mountains; nor made wars
With rocks, nor bold hands struck the World's
    strong bars,
Nor lost in too large bounds, our little Rome
Full sweetly with itself had dwelt at home.
My poor Alexis then, in peaceful life,
Had under some low roof loved his plain wife;
But now, ah me! from where he has no foes
He flies, and into wilful exile goes.
Cruel, return, or tell the reason why
Thy dearest parents have deserved to die.
And I, what is my crime I cannot tell,
Unless it be a crime t' have loved too well.
If heats of holier love and high desire
Make big thy fair breast with immortal fire,
What needs my virgin lord fly thus from me,
Who only wish his virgin wife to be?

Witness, chaste Heavens ! no happier vows I know
Than to a virgin grave untouch'd to go.
Love's truest knot by Venus is not tied ;
Nor do embraces only make a bride.
The Queen of angels [1] (and men chaste as you)
Was maiden-wife, and maiden-mother too.
Cecilia, [2] glory of her name and blood,
With happy gain her maiden vows made good.
The lusty bridegroom made approach—"Young
 man,
Take heed" (said she) "take heed, Valerian.
My bosom's guard, a spirit great and strong,
Stands arm'd to shield me from all wanton wrong.
My chastity is sacred ; and my Sleep
Wakeful, her dear vows undefiled to keep.
Pallas bears arms, forsooth ; and should there be
No fortress built for true Virginity ?
No gaping Gorgon this : none like the rest
Of your learn'd lies. Here you'll find no such jest.
I'm yours : O were my God, my Christ so too,
I'd know no name of Love on Earth but you."
He yields, and straight baptized, obtains the grace
To gaze on the fair soldier's glorious face.
Both mix'd at last their blood in one rich bed
Of rosy martyrdom, twice married.
O burn our Hymen bright in such high flame,
Thy torch, terrestrial Love, has here no name.
How sweet the mutual yoke of man and wife,
When holy fires maintain Love's heavenly life !

[1] Our Lady.
[2] A convert to Christianity, suffered martyrdom in 230
A.D. Married Valerian, a nobleman, whom she converted,
together with his brother Tiburtius. Both were martyred
a few days before St. Cecilia.

But I (so help me Heaven my hopes to see),
When thousands sought my love, loved none but
    thee.
Still, as their vain tears my firm vows did try,
" Alexis, he alone is mine " (said I).
Half true, alas ! half false, proves that poor line,
Alexis is alone ; but is not mine.

TRANSLATIONS

In the Praise of the Spring
(*Out of Virgil*[1])

A LL trees, all leafy groves confess the Spring
    Their gentlest friend ; then, then the lands
    begin
To swell with forward pride, and feed desire
To generation ; Heaven's Almighty Sire
Melts on the bosom of His love, and pours
Himself into her lap in fruitful showers,
And by a soft insinuation, mixed
With Earth's large mass, doth cherish and assist
Her weak conceptions ; no lone shade, but rings
With chatt'ring birds' delicious murmurings.
Then Venus' mild instinct (at set times) yields
The herds to kindly meetings, then the fields
(Quick with warm Zephyr's lively breath) lay forth
Their pregnant bosoms in a fragrant birth.
Each body's plump and juicy, all things full
Of supple moisture : no coy twig but will
Trust his belovèd blossom to the sun
(Grown lusty now) ; no vine so weak and young

[1] From Georgica ii. 323-345.   Ver adeo frondi
nemorum, ver utile silvis, etc.

That fears the foul-mouth'd Auster,[1] or those
    storms
That the South-west wind hurries in his arms,
But hastes her forward blossoms, and lays out,
Freely lays out her leaves ; nor do I doubt
But when the world first out of chaos sprang,
So smiled the days, and so the tenour ran
Of their felicity.   A Spring was there,
An everlasting Spring, the jolly year
Led round in his great circle ; no wind's breath
As then did smell of Winter, or of Death.
When Life's sweet light first shone on beasts, and
    when
From their hard mother Earth sprang hardy men ;
When beasts took up their lodging in the wood,
Stars in their higher chambers : never could
The tender growth of things endure the sense
Of such a change, but that the Heavens' indulgence
Kindly supplies sick Nature, and doth mould
A sweetly-temper'd mean, nor hot nor cold.

THE BEGINNING OF HELIODORUS [2]

THE smiling Morn had newly waked the Day,
And tipped the mountains with a tender ray :
When on a hill (whose high, imperious brow
Looks down, and sees the humble Nile below
Lick his proud feet, and haste into the seas
Through the great mouth that's named from
    Hercules)

[1] Sirocco
[2] From the Greek of Heliodorus. *Æthiopica*, Bk. 1
chap. i.

A band of men, rough as the arms they wore,
Look'd round, first to the sea, then to the shore:
The shore that show'd them what the sea denied—
Hope of a prey. There, to the mainland tied,
A ship they saw, no men she had, yet pressed
Appear'd with other lading, for her breast
Deep in the groaning waters wallowed
Up to the third ring; o'er the shore was spread
Death's purple triumph; on the blushing ground
Life's late forsaken houses all lay drown'd
In their own blood's dear deluge, some new dead,
Some panting in their yet warm ruins bled;
While their affrighted souls, now wing'd for flight,
Lent them the last flash of her glimmering light.
Those yet fresh streams, which crawlèd everywhere,
Showed that stern War had newly bathed him there.
Nor did the face of this disaster show
Marks of a fight alone, but feasting too:
A miserable and a monstrous feast,
Where hungry War had made himself a guest;
And, coming late, had eat up guests and all,
Who proved the feast to their own funeral, etc.

CUPID'S CRIER [1]

(Out of the Greek)

Love is lost, nor can his mother
Her little fugitive discover:
She seeks, she sighs, but nowhere spies him;
Love is lost, and thus she cries him:
    Oyez! if any happy eye
This roving wanton shall descry,

[1] From the Greek of Moschus.

Let the finder surely know
Mine is the wag; 'tis I that own
The wingèd wanderer; and that none
May think his labour vainly gone,
The glad descrier shall not miss
To taste the nectar of a kiss
From Venus' lips; but as for him
That brings him to me, he shall swim
In riper joys: more shall be his
(Venus assures him) than a kiss.
But lest your eye discerning slide,
These marks may be your judgment's guide:
His skin as with a fiery blushing
High-colour'd is; his eyes still flushing
With nimble flames; and though his mind
Be ne'er so curst, his tongue is kind:
For never were his words in aught
Found the pure issue of his thought.
The working bees' soft melting gold,
That which their waxen mines enfold,
Flows not so sweet as do the tones
Of his tuned accents; but if once
His anger kindle, presently
It boils out into cruelty
And fraud: he makes poor mortals' hurts
The objects of his cruel sports.
With dainty curls his froward face
Is crown'd about; but O, what place,
What farthest nook of lowest Hell
Feels not the strength, the reaching spell
Of his small hand? yet not so small
As 'tis powerful therewithal.
Though bare his skin, his mind he covers,
And like a saucy bird he hovers

With wanton wing, now here, now there,
'Bout men and women ; nor will spare
Till at length he perching rest,
In the closet of their breast.
His weapon is a little bow,
Yet such an one as (Jove knows how)
Ne'er suffer'd yet his little arrow
Of Heaven's high'st arches to fall narrow.
The gold that on his quiver smiles,
Deceives men's fears with flattering wiles :
But O ! (too well my wounds can tell)
With bitter shafts 'tis sauced too well.
He is all cruel, cruel all ;
His torch imperious, though but small,
Makes the sun, of flames the sire,
Worse than sun-burnt in his fire.
Wheresoe'er you chance to find him,
Seize him, bring him—but first bind him,
Pity not him, but fear thyself;
Though thou see the crafty elf
Tell down his silver drops unto thee :
They're counterfeit, and will undo thee.
With baited smiles if he display
His fawning cheeks, look not that way.
If he offer sugar'd kisses,
Start, and say, the serpent hisses.
Draw him, drag him, though he pray,
Woo, entreat, and crying say,
Prithee, sweet, now let me go,
Here's my quiver, shafts, and bow,
I'll give thee all, take all ; take heed
Lest his kindness make thee bleed.
    Whate'er it be Love offers, still presume
    That though it shines, 'tis fire, and will consume.

A Song

(Out of the Italian)

To thy lover
Dear, discover
That sweet blush of thine that shameth
(When those roses
It discloses)
All the flowers that Nature nameth.

In free air
Flow thy hair;
That no more Summer's best dresses
Be beholden
For their golden
Locks to Phœbus' flaming tresses.

O deliver
Love his quiver;
From thy eyes he shoots his arrows:
Where Apollo
Cannot follow:
Feather'd with his mother's sparrows.

O envy not
(That we die not)
Those dear lips whose door encloses
All the Graces
In their places,
Brother pearls, and sister roses,

From these treasures
Of ripe pleasures
One bright smile to clear the weather.

Earth and Heaven
Thus made even,
Both will be good friends together.

The air does woo thee,
Winds cling to thee;
Might a word once fly from out thee,
Storm and thunder
Would sit under,
And keep silence round about thee.

But if Nature's
Common creatures
So dear glories dare not borrow;
Yet thy beauty
Owes a duty
To my loving, lingering sorrow.

When to end me
Death shall send me
All his terrors to affright me:
Thine eyes' Graces
Gild their faces,
And those terrors shall delight me.

When my dying
Life is flying,
Those sweet airs that often slew me
Shall revive me,
Or reprieve me,
And to many deaths renew me.

(Out of the Italian)

Love now no fire hath left him,
　We two betwixt us have divided it.
Your eyes the light hath reft him,
　　The heat commanding in my heart doth sit.
　　　O that poor Love be not for ever spoiled,
　　　Let my heat to your light be reconciled.

So shall these flames, whose worth
　Now all obscurèd lies,
(Dressed in those beams) start forth
　And dance before your eyes.

Or else partake my flames
　(I care not whither),
And so in mutual names
　Of Love, burn both together.

(Out of the Italian)

Would any one the true cause find
How Love came nak't, a boy, and blind?
'Tis this: listening one day too long
To th' Syrens in my mistress' song,
The ecstasy of a delight
So much o'er-mastering all his might,
To that one sense made all else thrall,
And so he lost his clothes, eyes, heart, and
　all.

(Out of Catullus [1]*)*

COME and let us live, my dear,
Let us love and never fear
What the sourest fathers say :
Brightest Sol that dies to-day
Lives again as blithe to-morrow ;
But if we, dark sons of sorrow,
Set, O then how long a Night
Shuts the eyes of our short light !
Then let amorous kisses dwell
On our lips, begin and tell
A thousand, and a hundred score,
An hundred and a thousand more,
Till another thousand smother
That, and that wipe off another.
Thus at last, when we have numbered
Many a thousand, many a hundred,
We'll confound the reckoning quite,
And lose ourselves in wild delight :
While our joys so multiply
As shall mock the envious eye.

EPIGRAMS

UPON FORD'S TWO TRAGEDIES,
"LOVE'S SACRIFICE," AND "THE BROKEN HEART"

THOU cheat'st us, Ford ; mak'st one seem two
by art :
What is Love's Sacrifice but The Broken Heart ?

[1] Carm. v.

On Marriage

I would be married, but I'd have no wife ;
I would be married to a single life.

Upon the Fair Ethiopian sent to a Gentlewoman

Lo, here the fair Chariclia ! [1] in whom strove
So false a fortune, and so true a love !
Now, after all her toils by sea and land,
O may she but arrive at your white hand.
Her hopes are crown'd, only she fears that then
She shall appear true Ethiopian.

To Delia

(Out of Martial)

Four teeth thou hadst that rank'd in goodly state,
                    Kept thy mouth's gate.
The first blast of thy cough left two alone,
                    The second, none.
This last cough, Delia, cough'd out all thy fear,
Th' hast left the third cough now no business here.

Upon Venus putting on Mars's Arms

What ? Mars's sword ? fair Cytherea [2] say,
Why art thou armed so desperately to-day ?

[1] The lady love of Theagenes in the Greek romance,
" The loves of Theagenes and Charicleia," by Heliodorus,
Bishop of Trikka, 4th century.
[2] Venus.

Mars thou hast beaten naked, and, O then,
What need'st thou put on arms against poor men ?

UPON THE SAME

PALLAS saw Venus armed, and straight she cried,
" Come if thou dar'st, thus, thus let us be tried."
" Why, fool ! " says Venus, " thus provok'st thou
    me,
That being naked, thou know'st could conquer
    thee ? "

ON NANUS MOUNTED UPON AN ANT

HIGH mounted on an ant, Nanus the tall
Was thrown, alas ! and got a deadly fall :
Under th' unruly beast's proud feet he lies,
All torn ; with much ado yet ere he dies,
He strains these words : " Base Envy, do, laugh
    on,
Thus did I fall, and thus fell Phaethon."

TEMPERANCE, THE CHEAP
PHYSICIAN

(Upon the Translation of Lessius)

GO now, with some daring drug,
    Bait thy disease, and while they tug,
Thou, to maintain their cruel strife
Spend the dear treasure of thy life :
Go take physic, dote upon
Some big-named composition,—

The oraculous doctors' mystic bills,
Certain hard words made into pills;
And what at length shalt get by these?
Only a costlier disease.
Go poor man, think what shall be
Remedy 'gainst thy remedy.
That which makes us have no need
Of physic, that's physic indeed.
Hark hither, Reader: wouldst thou see
Nature her own physician be?
Wouldst see a man all his own wealth,
His own music, his own health?
A man, whose sober soul can tell
How to wear her garments well?
Her garments that upon her sit,
(As garments should do) close and fit?
A well-clothed soul, that's not oppress'd
Nor choked with what she should be dress'd?
Whose soul's sheath'd in a crystal shrine,
Through which all her bright features shine?
As when a piece of wanton lawn,
A thin aërial veil is drawn,
O'er Beauty's face; seeming to hide,
More sweetly shows the blushing bride:
A soul, whose intellectual beams
No mists do mask, no lazy steams?
A happy soul, that all the way
To Heaven, hath a Summer's day?
Wouldst see a man whose well-warm'd blood
Bathes him in a genuine flood?
A man, whose tunèd humours be
A set of rarest harmony?
Wouldst see blithe looks, fresh cheeks, beguile
'Age? Wouldst see December smile?

Wouldst see a nest of roses grow
In a bed of rev'rend snow?
Warm thoughts, free spirits, flattering
Winter's self into a Spring?
In sum, wouldst see a man that can
Live to be old, and still a man?
Whose latest, and most laden hours
Fall with soft wings, stuck with soft flowers;
And when Life's sweet fable ends,
His soul and body part like friends:
No quarrels, murmurs, no delay:
A kiss, a sigh, and so away?
This rare one, Reader, wouldst thou see,
Hark hither: and thyself be he!

CRASHAW'S ANSWER FOR HOPE [1]

DEAR Hope! Earth's dow'ry, and Heaven's
    debt!
The entity of things that are not yet.
Subtlest, but surest being! thou by whom
Our nothing has a definition!
    Substantial shade! whose sweet allay
    Blends both the noons of Night and Day:
    Fates cannot find out a capacity
    Of hurting thee.
From thee their lean dilemma, with blunt horn,
Shrinks as the sick moon from the wholesome morn.

    Rich hope! Love's legacy, under lock
Of Faith!—still spending, and still growing stock!

[1] This was written in answer to a poem by Cowley
beginning, "Hope, whose weak being ruined is."

Our crown-land lies above, yet each meal brings
A seemly portion for the sons of kings.
   Nor will the virgin-joys we wed
   Come less unbroken to our bed,
   Because that from the bridal cheek of Bliss,
   Thou steal'st us down a distant kiss.
Hope's chaste stealth harms no more Joy's
    maidenhead
Than spousal rites prejudge the marriage-bed.

   Fair hope! our earlier Heav'n! by thee
Young time is taster to Eternity:
Thy generous wine with age grows strong, not
   sour,
Nor does it kill thy fruit, to smell thy flower.
   Thy golden growing head never hangs down,
   Till in the lap of Love's full noon
   It falls; and dies! O no, it melts away
   As doth the dawn into the Day:
As lumps of sugar loose themselves, and twine
Their subtle essence with the soul of wine.

   Fortune? alas, above the World's low wars
Hope walks and kicks the curl'd heads of con-
   spiring stars.
Her keel cuts not the waves where our winds stir,
Fortune's whole lottery is one blank to her.
   Her shafts and she fly far above,
   And forage in the fields of light and love.
   Sweet Hope! kind cheat! fair fallacy! by thee
   We are not where nor what we be,
But what and where we would be. Thus art thou
Our absent presence, and our future now.

Faith's sister! nurse of fair desire!
Fear's antidote! a wise and well-staid fire!
Temper 'twixt chill Despair, and torrid Joy!
Queen regent in young Love's minority!
  Though the vext chymic vainly chases
  His fugitive gold through all her faces;
  Though Love's more fierce, more fruitless fires
    assay:
  One face more fugitive than all they;
True Hope's a glorious huntress, and her chase,
The God of Nature in the fields of grace.

CRASHAW'S MOTTO

LIVE, Jesus, live, and let it be
My life to die for love of Thee.

INDEX TO FIRST LINES

	Page
A Brook, whose stream so great, so good . .	181
A drop, one drop, how sweetly one fair drop .	143
A plant of noble stem, forward and fair. . .	170
All Hybla's honey, all that sweetness can . .	147
All trees, all leafy groves confess the Spring. .	200
All we have is God's, and yet	146
And now thou'rt set wide ope, the spears' sad art .	146
As if the storm meant Him	153
Bright Babe, Whose awful beauties make . .	59
Britain, the mighty Ocean's lovely bride . .	188
Christ bids the dumb tongue speak ; it speaks, the sound	148
Come and let us live, my dear	208
Come death, come bonds, nor do you shrink, my ears	146
Come, ye shepherds, whose blest sight . . .	50
Could not once blinding me, cruel, suffice . .	151
Dear, Heaven designèd soul	107
Dear Hope ! Earth's dowry, and Heaven's debt .	212
Dear relics of a dislodged soul, whose lack . .	179
Death, what dost ? O, hold thy blow . . .	171
Each blest drop on each blest limb . . .	145
Eternal Love ! what 'tis to love Thee well . .	152
Faithless and fond Mortality	168
Four teeth thou hadst that rank'd in goodly state .	209
Go now, with some daring drug	210
Go, smiling souls, your new-built cages break .	147
Hail, most high, most humble one . . .	135
Hail, sister springs	3
Happy, me ! O happy sheep	46
Hark ! she is called, the parting hour is come .	123

215

                                                              Page
Hath only Anger an omnipotence 142
Hear'st thou, my soul, what serious things .   . 128
Her eyes' flood licks His feet's fair stain   .   . 148
Here, where our Lord once laid His head   .   . 152
High mounted on an ant, Nanus the tall   .   . 210
How fit our well-ranked feasts do follow   .   . 151
How life and death in Thee 152
I, late the Roman youths' loved praise and pride . 195
I paint so ill, my piece had need to be   .   . 167
I sing the name which none can say   .   . 38
I would be married, but I'd have no wife   .   . 209
If ever Pity were acquainted   .   .   . 174
In shade of Death's sad tree 12
Is murder no sin ? or a sin so cheap   .   . 150
Jesu, no more ! It is full tide   .   .   . 36
Know you, fair, on what you look   .   . 110
Know'st thou this, Soldier ? 'tis a much changed
     plant, which yet 152
Let hoary Time's vast bowels be the grave   .   . 186
Let it no longer be a forlorn-hope   .   . 149
Live, Jesus live, and let it be   .   .   . 214
Lo, here a little volume, but great book   .   . 103
Lo, here the fair Chariclia ! in whom strove .   . 209
Look up, languishing soul ! Lo, where the fair   . 32
Lord, by Thy sweet and saving sign   .   . 19
Lord, what is man ? why should he cost Thee   . 132
Lord, when the sense of Thy sweet grace   .   . 123
Love, brave Virtue's younger Brother   .   . 184
Love is lost, nor can his mother   .   .   . 202
Love now no fire hath left him   .   .   . 207
Love, thou art absolute sole lord   .   . 111
'Midst all the dark and knotty snares   .   . 34
'Mongst those long rows of crowns that gild your
     race   58
Muse, now the servant of soft loves no more   . 71
No roofs of gold o'er riotous tables shining   . 109
Now, Lord, or never, they'll believe on Thee   . 143
Now westward Sol had spent the richest beams   . 157
O mighty Nothing ! unto thee   .   .   . 144
O these wakeful wounds of Thine   .   . 35
On the proud banks of great Euphrates' flood   . 48

Page

One eye? a thousand rather, and a thousand more . 145
Pallas saw Venus armed, and straight she cried . 210
Passenger, whoe'er thou art 176
Rich churlish Land, that hid'st so long in thee . 198
Rich Lazarus! richer in those gems, thy tears . 143
Rise heir of fresh Eternity 70
Rise, royal Sion! rise and sing . . . 99
Rise, then, immortal maid, Religion, rise . . 126
Rise, thou best and brightest morning . . . 55
See here an easy feast that knows no wound . 143
Seen? and yet hated Thee? they did not see . 145
Show me Himself, Himself (bright Sir), O show . 151
So I may gain Thy death my life I'll give . . 151
Take these, Time's tardy truants, sent by me . 194
Tell me, bright boy, tell me, my golden lad . . 142
That on her lap she casts her humble eye . 146
The modest front of this small floor . . 177
The smiling Morn had newly waked the Day . 201
The world's Light shines; shine as it will . 149
These Hours, and that which hovers o'er my end . 31
They have left Thee naked, Lord; O that they had 153
This reverend shadow cast that setting sun . . 168
Thou cheatest us, Ford; mak'st one seem two by
  art 208
Thou hast the art on't, Peter, and canst tell . . 143
Thou spak'st the word (Thy word's a law) . 144
Thou trimm'st a Prophet's tomb, and dost be—
  queath 149
Thou water turn'st to wine (fair friend of life) . 145
Though all the joys I had fled hence with thee . 197
Thus have I back again to thy bright name . 117
Thy God was making haste into thy roof . . 144
Thy hands are washed, but O, the water's spilt . 150
To see both blended in one flood . . . 147
To Thee these first-fruits of My growing death . 56
To these, whom Death again did wed . . . 179
To thy lover 205
Two devils at one blow Thou hast laid flat . 147
Two mites, two drops (yet all her house and land) 144
Two went to pray! O, rather say . . . 142
Under thy shadow may I lurk awhile . . . 151

	Page
Welcome, my grief, my joy; how dear's . . 148	
Well, Peter, dost thou wield thy active sword . 150	
Well-meaning readers, you that come as friends . 119	
What bright soft thing is this 16	
What Heaven-besiegèd heart is this . . . 136	
What Heaven-entreated heart is this . . . 139	
What ? Mars' sword ?. fair Cytherea say . 209	
What succour can I hope the Muse will send . 182	
Whatever story of their cruelty 154	
When.you are mistress of the song . . . 187	
Where art thou, Sol, while thus the blindfold Day 181	
Whoe'er she be 162	
Why dost thou wound my wounds, O thou that passest by 148	
With all the powers my poor heart hath . . 97	
Would any one the true cause find 207	

PRINTED BY MORRISON AND GIBB LIMITED, EDINBURGH

A PROSPECTUS

OF

THE LITTLE LIBRARY

I PROTEST that I am devoted to no school in particular: I condemn no school, I reject none. I am for the school of all the great men. I care for Wordsworth as well as for Byron, for Burns as well as Shelley, for Boccaccio as well as for Milton, for Bunyan as well as Rabelais, for Cervantes as much as for Dante, for Corneille as well as for Shakespeare, for Goldsmith as well as Goethe. I stand by the sentence of the world.

FREDERIC HARRISON

METHUEN & CO.
36 Essex Street, W.C.

THE LITTLE LIBRARY

Pott 8vo. Each Vol., cloth, 1s. 6d. net; leather, 2s. 6d. net

MESSRS METHUEN intend to produce a series of small books under the above title, containing some of the famous works in English and other literatures, in the domains of fiction, poetry, and belles lettres. The series will also contain several volumes of selections in prose and verse.

The books will be edited with the most sympathetic and scholarly care. Each one, where it seems desirable, will contain an introduction which will give (1) a short biography of the author, (2) a critical estimate of the book. Where they are necessary, short notes will be added at the foot of the page.

The Little Library will ultimately contain complete sets of the novels of W. M. Thackeray, Jane Austen, the sisters Brontë, Mrs Gaskell, and others. It will also contain the best work of many other novelists whose names are household words.

Each volume will have a photogravure frontispiece, and the books will be produced with great care in a style uniform with that of The Library of Devotion.

On the opposite page is printed a first list of books, and many others are in preparation.

The First Volumes will be—

Vanity Fair. By W. M. THACKERAY. Edited by Stephen Gwynn. *Three Volumes.*

Pendennis. By W. M. THACKERAY. Edited by Stephen Gwynn. *Three Volumes.*

Pride and Prejudice. By JANE AUSTEN. Edited by E. V. Lucas. *Two Volumes.*

Cranford. By MRS GASKELL. Edited by E. V. Lucas.

John Halifax, Gentleman. By MRS CRAIK. Edited by Annie Matheson. *Two Volumes.*

Lavengro. By GEORGE BORROW. Edited by F. H. Groome. *Two Volumes.*

Eothen. By A. W. KINGLAKE. Edited by D.

A Little Book of English Lyrics.

A Little Book of Scottish Verse. Edited by T. F. Henderson.

The Inferno of Dante. Translated by H. F. CARY. With an Introduction and Notes by Paget Toynbee.

The Early Poems of Alfred, Lord Tennyson. Edited by J. Churton Collins, M.A.

The Princess, and other Poems. By ALFRED, LORD TENNYSON. Edited by Elizabeth Wordsworth.

Maud, and other Poems. By ALFRED, LORD TENNYSON. Edited by Elizabeth Wordsworth.

In Memoriam. By ALFRED, LORD TENNYSON. Edited by H. C. Beeching.

Selected Poems of William Blake. Edited by Mark Perugini.

Sedley, but she swallowed her mortification as
well as she had the abominable curry before it,
and as soon as she could speak, said, with a
comical, good-humoured air—

"I ought to have remembered the pepper
which the Princess of Persia puts in the cream-
tarts in the *Arabian Nights.* Do you put
cayenne into your cream-tarts in India, sir?"

Old Sedley began to laugh, and thought Rebecca
was a good-humoured girl. Joseph simply said—
"Cream-tarts, Miss? Our cream is very bad
in Bengal. We generally use goat's milk; and,
'gad, do you know, I've got to prefer it!"

"You won't like *everything* from India now,
Miss Sharp," said the old gentleman; but when
the ladies had retired after dinner, the wily old
fellow said to his son, "Have a care, Joe; that
girl is setting her cap at you."

"Pooh! nonsense!" said Joe, highly flattered.
"I recollect, sir, there was a girl at Dumdum, a
daughter of Cutler of the Artillery, and after-
wards married to Lance, the surgeon, who made
a dead set at me in the year '4—at me and
Mulligatawney, whom I mentioned to you before
dinner—a devilish good fellow Mulligatawney—
he's a magistrate at Budgebudge, and sure to be
in council in five years. Well, sir, the Artillery
gave a ball, and Quintin, of the King's 14th,
said to me, 'Sedley,' said he, 'I bet you thirteen
to ten that Sophy Cutler hooks either you or
Mulligatawney before the rains.' 'Done,' says
I; and egad, sir—this claret's very good.
Adamson's or Carbonell's? . . ."

A slight snore was the only reply: the honest
stockbroker was asleep, and so the rest of Joseph's

[*Specimen Page*]

106
102.36
104
104.16
112.32
116.50
120.66
124.82
128.98
133.52
138.04
144.30
150 —
156 —
162.24

100
.04
4.80

129
.04
$16